INSERVICE EDUCATION

for Content Area Teachers

by
Mary Dunn Siedow
North Carolina State University

David M. Memory
Indiana State University

Page S. Bristow
University of Delaware

Published by the
INTERNATIONAL READING ASSOCIATION
800 Barksdale Road, Box 8139
Newark, Delaware 19714

Copyright 1985 by the
International Reading Association, Inc.

Library of Congress Cataloging in Publication Data

Siedow, Mary Dunn.
   Inservice education for content area teachers.

   Includes bibliographies.
   1. Teachers — Inservice training — United States.   2.
Reading — Teacher training — United States.   3. Reading
comprehension — Teacher training — United States.
I. Memory, David M.   II. Bristow, Page S.   III. Title
LB1731.S5225   1985   371.1'46'0973   85-8228
ISBN 0-87207-960-0

Contents

The International Reading Association attempts, through its publications, to provide a forum for a wide spectrum of opinion on reading. This policy permits divergent viewpoints without assuming the endorsement of the Association.

Foreword

Helping inservice leaders to help content area teachers on the job to improve in teaching students how to read and understand content related material is the major purpose of this publication. Teachers of history, science, mathematics, or any of the many other content areas view themselves as teachers of a specific content—and that is as it should be. Nevertheless, students in most content courses must read textbooks, references, and other printed materials related to topics in those courses. Content area teachers have the major responsibility for instructing these students in content reading strategies.

The authors of *Inservice Education for Content Area Teachers* emphasize that this publication is written in recognition that content area teachers are sufficiently different from other teachers to warrant special attention in inservice activities. They also emphasize the importance of inservice education for content area teachers since so few of them take courses in content area reading. Their model for inservice begins with an assessment of staff needs and ends with an evaluation of inservice effectiveness, followed by follow-up assistance and reinforcement. That model reflects the view that inservice should be based on real needs of those who are being helped, the help should be systematic, the effectiveness of inservice activities should be evaluated, and follow-up assistance should be provided.

This practical publication contains numerous suggestions for use in planning, carrying out, and evaluating the effectiveness of inservice aimed toward helping content area teachers improve their effectiveness in teaching reading related skills. Among the aids in the booklet are checklists, assessment instruments, attitude inventories, lists of instructional practices related to reading in content areas, lists of content area reading skills categorized into 14 subject areas (as art, science, mathematics, home economics, social studies), and a list of reading related objectives with suggestions for evaluation procedures appropriate for each. In Chapter 3, over 350 articles and books are listed as resources for the development of student learning strategies. Most of these references are categorized under approximately 40 topics—almost any topic anyone could possibly need in content area reading instruction. More than 250 references, categorized into 14 subject areas, are presented in Chapter 4. Both lists contain brief annotations for each reference, thus making them extremely valuable resources for directors of inservice activities for content area teachers.

This publication should appeal to all persons interested in inservice in the area of reading for content area teachers. The authors have prepared a thoughtful and useful booklet.

Ira E. Aaron, *President*
International Reading Association
1983-1984

Chapter One

Inservice Education for Content Area Teachers: Some Basic Principles

Mary Dunn Siedow

Why a Monograph on Inservice in Content Area Reading?

Given the abundance of professional literature on inservice education, it might seem superfluous to address ourselves to a single
population of teachers and to a specific topic. However, experience
as teachers and consultants, including microworkshops (conducted
at IRA conventions) on inservice education in content area reading,
has convinced us that participants in those workshops already knew
from daily experience that 1) there are some peculiar aspects of
content area teaching which make the task of providing appropriate
reading inservice difficult and challenging, 2) content area teachers
have specific needs regarding content area reading which are best
met via inservice education, and 3) there are few available resources
which specifically address the subject of content reading inservice.

Content area teachers are subject specialists who have chosen to share their interest in subject matter with students. Their
preparation for teaching has been virtually subject specific, giving
them little exposure to general instructional methodology. They
work in schools where departmental organization separates them
from one another, reinforcing the belief that the differences among
content areas are more pervasive than are the commonalities. Often
they are faced with students who do not share their teachers'
interests in subject matter, who do not challenge their teachers'
positions, or who are not prepared to deal with concepts presented.
Under such conditions is it any wonder that content area teachers
conclude that the problem lies outside their specialization? They

1

know what they have been prepared to do; whatever else needs to be done must belong to someone else's specialty.

One aspect of instruction for which content area teachers often are not prepared is that of reading. Despite the widespread growth of interest in content area reading over the past 15 years, there are still large numbers of content area teachers who have had little or no formal preparation in this aspect of instructional methodology. The number of states which require a content area reading methods course for secondary teaching certification has grown considerably since Austin (1968) reported that such a requirement was virtually nonexistent. Bader (1975) reported that 18 of 50 states and the District of Columbia (35 percent) require a reading course for either temporary or permanent certification of secondary teachers. Thomas and Simpson (1979) reported that 28 states have some kind of content reading requirement for certification. More recent surveys (Thomas & Simpson, 1979; IRA, 1981; and Thompson, 1982) show that more than 70 percent of the states have a reading requirement for secondary teachers. In the most recent survey, Thompson (1982) reported that of the 29 states with a reading requirement, 22 (76 percent) extend that requirement to all content area teachers. Given that most of these certification requirements are relatively recent, it can be concluded that a large percentage of new secondary teachers have never had a course in the teaching of content area reading, and that many veteran teachers completed their education before content reading courses were available.

There appears to be a general lack of preparedness on the part of content area teachers to incorporate reading instruction into content lessons. The recency and the limited nature of certification requirements help to explain the lack of preparedness on the part of content area teachers to provide reading assistance to students. The specialization and eventual isolation of teachers described above may be a second explanation. Teachers may have tried the general strategies learned in content area reading classes and then abandoned them because they were not wholly and consistently applicable or because the teachers could not make transfers from general method to specific content (Askov & Dupuis, 1979). Teachers who believe themselves isolated and ill prepared to deal with subjects outside their specializations may reject the notion that some things are generally applicable. Whatever the explanation, there is still a great need among content area teachers for knowledge of the reading process and of how to help students to improve as readers, a need which essentially must be met through inservice education.

In most cases content area teachers prove to be a tough audience for inservice presenters. Insulated by their commitment to content and by their belief that students should enter classes prepared to deal maturely with subject matter, such teachers often must be convinced that they have a need to learn about strategies for improving students' reading. Their reluctance to take on new instructional responsibilities must be replaced by motivation to try new techniques.

The task of providing inservice education in content area reading contains several challenging elements. Few resources exist which specifically address inservice in content area reading. Teachers must be convinced that there is a need to learn about strategies for improving reading and they must become motivated to learn and apply new techniques. The gap between general strategies and specific content must be bridged so that the former can be fully implemented in the latter. All must be presented in a way which is intellectually credible, stimulating to adults and in accord with adult learning styles.

This monograph was developed to meet the challenges outlined above. A simple model of inservice education was selected and is described here because it is generalizable and appropriate across content areas. The steps of the model have been illustrated with descriptions and examples of content area reading inservice sessions. References to articles applying content reading strategies to specific content areas have been provided. In so doing, the reading related needs of content area teachers are addressed. This monograph is intended to be a resource for administrators, supervisors, and others who are charged with providing inservice in reading for content area teachers.

Principles for Content Area Reading Inservice

Some of the authors' views on inservice in content area reading have already been voiced. Content area teachers must realize a need to learn about content reading strategies, and they must be motivated to employ the strategies in their classrooms if the inservice is to have any lasting effects. Teachers who will be participants in inservice should play critical roles in every aspect of inservice, from voicing their needs initially through participating in sessions to engaging in follow-up activities once the training is completed. The practical needs of content teachers and their students should be determined early. These needs should be the basis for planning and conducting inservice sessions and for evaluation and follow-up activities.

A model of inservice based on the above general guidelines would require several specific principles as well. Those which govern the model used in this monograph follow.

1. An assessment of the needs of participants should form the basis of the inservice program. This process should begin with the establishment of a coordinator or a coordinating committee and should include activities designed to identify the needs of participants, their students, supervisors, and administrators, who will benefit from inservice.

2. Objectives for inservice should be developed based on the needs of participants and their students. They should be formulated both in terms of the ultimate outcomes for students and the immediate outcomes related to teacher practices.

3. Content of sessions should be based on objectives established from needs assessment. This content should include relevant and potentially effective instructional strategies which stand a reasonable chance of being successfully implemented in classrooms.

4. Methods of presenting content and staffing for sessions should involve teachers as adults responsible for their own learning. Modeling of strategies applied to specific content areas, opportunities for reflection on ideas, and discussions of relative merits of strategies are all methods by which adults learn and become willing to try new ideas and strategies. Such methods could be presented successfully by experienced teachers, university professors, or consultants selected for their expertise in aspects of reading being considered.

5. Evaluation of individual sessions and of long term programs is essential to measure accomplishment of objectives and also to assess further needs of participants.

6. Follow-up activities should be conducted to extend techniques learned and to modify them as needed in specific

situations. Meetings between individual participants and presenters, small group discussions, and reunion sessions of participants can all be used to insure that inservice has lasting effects.

These principles form a logical and reasonable basis for a model of inservice education. They are in concert with the findings of recent studies of effective inservice education as collected and interpreted by Hutson (1981).

A Model for Content Area Reading Inservice

A model which incorporates the specific principles outlined can serve as a useful tool for planning and conducting reading inservice for content area teachers. Such a model is illustrated below. It is a model which is simple and probably familiar to inservice leaders, and one which can be used successfully with content area teachers.

There are some implications of the model which should be discussed. It should be obvious that any inservice which follows this model will be a long term effort. Successful infusion of reading instruction into content areas takes time; content area teachers need time to consider, attempt, and modify new practices. The efficacy of a long term approach is documented by Diem, Schnitz, and Fairweather (1981) and by the success of the Network of Secondary School Demonstration Centers for Teaching Reading in Content Areas directed for the past several years by Nelson and Herber (1982).

Another implication of the model can be seen in its design. It will be noted that while the elements of the model were first outlined in linear fashion, their arrangement here is cyclical, interactive, continuous. Each step taken leads to the next, and the final step in one sequence leads to the beginning of a new sequence. Thus, what content area teachers learn about reading from inservice sessions will be developmental. At every step, interactions among participants, presenters, and coordinators produce feedback which insures that inservice sessions are on the track and allows modifications when and where they are needed.

A final implication of the model is that its successful execution requires the cooperative involvement of teachers, administrators, and inservice coordinators and committees. Teachers should

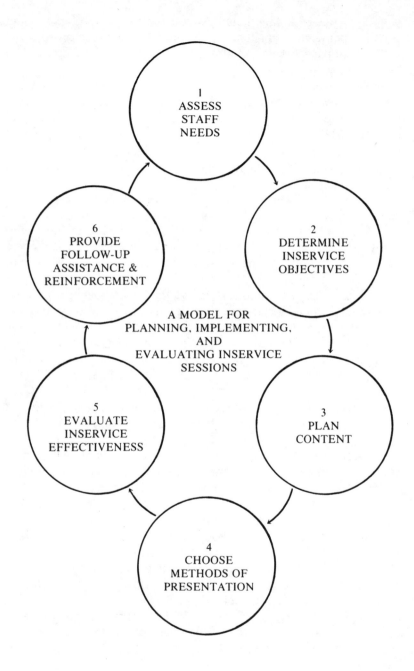

A MODEL FOR
PLANNING, IMPLEMENTING,
AND
EVALUATING INSERVICE
SESSIONS

1
ASSESS
STAFF
NEEDS

2
DETERMINE
INSERVICE
OBJECTIVES

3
PLAN
CONTENT

4
CHOOSE
METHODS OF
PRESENTATION

5
EVALUATE
INSERVICE
EFFECTIVENESS

6
PROVIDE
FOLLOW-UP
ASSISTANCE &
REINFORCEMENT

be motivated to participate enthusiastically and to implement strategies learned in their classrooms. Administrators, especially principals, should provide support and, whenever possible, participate actively in inservice. Coordinators and committees should take care to assure that inservice is well designed and executed to meet participants' needs.

In the remaining chapters of this monograph, individual aspects of the model will be discussed. While each aspect is considered separately, inservice coordinators and presenters are urged to remember that commitment to the integrated total model is the key to successful inservice.

References

Askov, Eunice N., & Mary M. Dupuis. "Guidelines for Inservice Programs to Teach Reading in Content Areas," *Journal of Teacher Education*, 1979, *30*, 16-18.

Austin, Mary C. "Professional Training of Reading Personnel," *Innovation and Change in Reading Instruction*, NSSE. Chicago: University of Chicago Press, 1968, 357-396.

Bader, Lois A. "Certification Requirements in Reading: A Trend," *Journal of Reading*, 1975, *19*, 237-240.

Certification Requirements in Reading, third edition. Newark, Delaware: International Reading Association, 1981.

Diem, Richard A., James E. Schnitz, & Peter G. Fairweather. "Reading Program for Secondary Teachers: An Evaluation of an Inservice Model," *High School Journal*, 1981, *65*, 13-22.

Hutson, Harry M., Jr. "Inservice Best Practices: The Learnings of General Education," *Journal of Research and Development in Education*, 1981, *14*, 1-10.

Nelson, Joan, & Harold L. Herber. "A Perspective on Two Years," *Network News* (Newsletter of the Network of Secondary School Demonstration Centers for Teaching Reading in Content Areas), 1982, *2*, 4.

Thomas, Keith J., & Michele Simpson. "Reading Requirements and Basic Secondary Teacher Certification: An Update," *Reading Horizons*, 1979, *20*, 20-26.

Thompson, Stephen J. "Secondary Teacher Certification Requirements in Reading: An Update," *Journal of Reading Education*, 1982, *9*, 19-24.

Chapter Two

Assessing Needs

Mary Dunn Siedow

A significant finding of two major reviews of research on staff development (Berman & McLaughlin, 1978; Lawrence, 1974) is that successful inservice programs are most likely to result from training which addresses the individual needs of participants. The effects of inservice are likely to be more lasting when teachers are allowed to ask for the kinds of inservice they need and to participate actively throughout the inservice series. Determination of the needs of teachers is, therefore, a critical initial phase of an inservice series.

The model of inservice education proposed in this monograph begins with needs assessment, generally considered to be an essential part of staff development and certainly vital to a program which must serve professionals representing a variety of subject fields. By assessing needs of participants, inservice coordinators can determine what will constitute appropriate inservice sessions. By drawing teachers into participatory roles in the planning of inservice sessions, coordinators can develop the involvement necessary for successful inservice.

Needs assessment has been described as a means of finding the gaps between what is and what ought to be (Wood, Thompson & Russell, 1981). Descriptions such as this have made needs assessment an accepted part of most inservice models. Such descriptions, however, do not delineate the parameters of needs assessment. Efforts to find ill defined gaps may result in needs assessment which is too broad or too narrow to address teachers' needs, or to be useful in setting priorities. In order to be appropriate for a particular situation, needs assessment must find the right number of the right gaps between what exists and what could and should exist in a school.

Appropriate needs assessment requires informed examination of existing conditions, reasoned projections of desirable goals, and careful meshing of the two. In the content areas, informed examination means looking at all content conditions—those which are specific to one area and those which cross several areas. It means creating awareness that there are some undesirable aspects of existing conditions, and that teachers have the potential to become more effective. It means creating in teachers a sense of commitment to full participation in the inservice program. Once teachers and coordinators recognize what special and general conditions exist, they are likely to be able to develop reasonable goals and to suggest ways in which these goals are appropriate for meeting their needs.

Appropriate needs assessment for content area reading inservice is most likely to result when it involves those who will participate in and benefit from the sessions. This means teachers, supervisors, administrators, and presenters. Each group of individuals is likely to have ideas to contribute; each is likely to provide a viewpoint from which others will benefit. The quality of the needs assessment, and therefore of the inservice series, will be enhanced by the involvement of all groups (Johnson & Yeakey, 1977).

Bringing together a group of teachers, supervisors, administrators, and presenters requires some effort. Initially, the impetus might come from any of the individuals involved. A group of teachers, for example, might approach a district's inservice coordinator to request assistance. A reading supervisor might identify an area of need and bring together teachers and inservice coordinators to work out a means of meeting that need. The availability of a certain presenter might spark the interest of teachers. Once interest is indicated, it should be carefully nurtured so that an inservice series can be developed.

To facilitate needs assessment and the other aspects of inservice education, a person is needed who can act as a leader and as a resource. A district's inservice coordinator would be the obvious choice, but where no such person exists, a supervisor or qualified teacher might assume the role. Inservice coordinators should be individuals with considerable expertise in content area reading. They will be responsible for guiding the inservice series, for keeping participants and presenters on the job, and for taking charge of managerial tasks. They must be prepared to exercise their leadership at any time in the series when conditions require it.

Many school faculties appoint a committee whose job it is to see that the original enthusiasm for inservice is carried through the sessions, evaluation, and follow up. This reading committee's size and makeup may vary, but generally it includes teachers, one or more supervisors, and perhaps an outside consultant who might be a major presenter also. The committee handles administrative details, sees to it that sessions are held as planned, and monitors teachers' changing attitudes and needs so that the inservice program can continually meet those needs.

Inservice coordinators and committees begin their tasks with needs assessment. They must develop needs assessment instruments from preliminary objectives which they develop. They must conduct activities with teachers which are designed to interest them in the proposed inservice series.

Where content area teachers are concerned, needs assessment is particularly important. Unless a careful needs assessment is carried out, there is no way to provide inservice which is appropriate across content areas. Because content area teachers represent a variety of subject specialties and levels of experience, they must be approached in ways related to those subjects and that experience. Teachers in each content area must understand that reading is related to their classrooms and is not a specialty topic for some other class. They must become acquainted with the concepts of shared need and shared responsibility, understanding that reading is a process which crosses disciplines, belongs to all, and cannot be compartmentalized. Needs assessment really has two goals: 1) development of motivation and commitment on the part of teachers, and 2) use of appropriate procedures to try to reach consensus about what is needed. In the first part of this chapter, the use of needs assessment to motivate teachers toward consensus will be discussed. In the second part of the chapter, alternative needs assessment instruments will be illustrated.

Developing Motivation and Commitment

Content area teachers must be motivated to participate in an inservice program and to commit themselves to implementing the reading strategies learned there in their classrooms. Inservice coordinators can begin to develop motivation and commitment in the introductory activities designed to acquaint teachers with content area reading. Here, the existing expertise of teachers can be used as a demonstration of their potential for learning to incorporate reading strategies into their instructional repertoires. Small seeds of dissatisfaction can be seen, so that teachers can recognize unsuccessful aspects of classroom instruction and realize that they are capable of modifying their own behaviors and those of their students. A delicate balance must be maintained among the elements of teacher expertise, belief in self, dissatisfaction, and realization of potential. Out of such a balance will come a sense of commitment to the goals of the inservice program.

The ultimate goal of needs assessment is reaching consensus. To whatever degree is possible, teachers, supervisors, and presenters should agree on those things which are needed and desirable. They should also agree on the program by which they will attain the goals they outline from the results of needs assessment.

In many cases it will not be possible to reach full consensus on all points. When this occurs, coordinators or committee members must take care not to let interest dissipate. They should exercise leadership, using their own expertise to judge areas of need or to suggest ways of resolving apparent disagreements. Those areas of need upon which there is consensus should be highlighted, and goals should be developed for initial inservice sessions. There should be general understanding that needs assessment activities will be taken up again once the sessions are under way, possibly in combination with evaluation of initial sessions. After one or two sessions, participants will have learned some things about content area reading and may well have modified their views about their own needs. Interim assessment can help to resolve early disagreement and may help to reach further consensus so that later sessions can be planned. A few words of caution—when needs assessment is broken off in this way, it is a good idea to set an early time for the interim needs assessment. Conducting interim needs assessment concurrently with evaluation of early sessions assures that the total inservice series can progress continuously. The inservice coordinator and committee must take active leadership roles so that their expertise can help guide the needs assessment. Often what appear to be vast differences between people can be ameliorated by the infusion of information by a knowledgeable leader.

Needs Assessment Instruments

Once it has been decided that a needs assessment will be conducted, it becomes necessary to determine the form needs assessment will take. There are several types of instruments which can be developed or modified for use with a particular group of content area teachers. There are checklists, questionnaires, dual scale checklists for rating "what is" versus "what ought to be," and multiphase structured discussion strategies. Selecting, modifying, or developing an instrument for a particular group of teachers must be done carefully and thoughtfully.

Developing Checklists and Questionnaires

Often an inservice coordinator or committee decides to develop a needs assessment instrument for a particular group of content area teachers. The first task is to compile a list of topics which can be used as items. These items should mirror the kinds of objectives which will be written for inservice. In Chapter 3 five levels of objectives will be discussed: teacher beliefs, teacher abilities, teacher practices, student behaviors, and student learning. Chapter 3 contains lists of sample abilities related to these levels of objectives. Coordinators or committees developing needs assessment instruments could use these lists and ideas from Chapter 3 to generate items for their instruments. Items from the lists are used in the examples below.

Checklists and questionnaires are common forms of needs assessment instruments. The two share many characteristics and, in fact, differ mainly in format. Checklists consist of phrases and require participants to indicate choices by checking alternatives described. Questionnaires consist of questions to which participants respond, sometimes openly and other times in prescribed alternatives. The more important differences lie within the two formats. Some checklists and questionnaires are open and allow free responses. Others require participants to rank choices or to respond on multiple scales, thus providing information about both the range and priority of needs.

When free expression of individuals' needs or beliefs is desired, an open ended questionnaire might be used. Questions are presented with spaces for responses and may address any of the levels of objectives discussed in Chapter 3. A question such as

"What are some things you would like to be able to do to improve your students' comprehension of their textbooks?" might elicit needed teacher abilities. A question such as "What are some things you would like your students to do when they encounter unknown words?" might suggest some student learning which needs to be developed. Either of these sample questions is likely to elicit responses at more than one level of objectives. Teachers might suggest that they need to develop strategies to help students comprehend (teacher ability), or they may suggest that they need to employ known strategies more consistently (teacher practice). In responding to the question on student behaviors, teachers might also suggest that they need to develop strategies (teacher abilities) or model strategies (teacher practices) in order for students to employ them. Inservice coordinators who use open questionnaires must be prepared to analyze responses carefully, and to categorize them so that appropriate objectives can be developed.

Open checklists are probably the simplest instruments to use. A list of possible inservice topics is developed from the objectives in Chapter 3. This list is arranged as a checklist and presented to teachers who are directed to check those topics which are of greatest interest or need for them. Those topics which receive the largest numbers of checks become the focus of inservice sessions.

Figure 1. Excerpt from a sample checklist (student abilities).

Check the abilities with which you would like to provide better assistance to your students.

_____ Learning unfamiliar words
_____ Using context clues
_____ Using structural clues
_____ Making inferences
_____ Recognizing main ideas
_____ Conducting library research

In the sample checklist items, several basic aspects of the reading process are named. By checking items, teachers would indicate areas in which they hope to improve their instructional techniques in order to effect changes in student behavior.

The sample items also illustrate some of the problems which arise from the use of simple checklists. Sometimes the topics are vague and are misunderstood by content area teachers. Some teachers check most or all of the topics, shopping list fashion; other teachers check very few. Individual teachers' priorities are not considered, making it possible for a topic of interest with low priority to receive enough votes to be used as a session topic. These problems are solved to some extent by modifications in the checklist format.

A simple modification would be to ask teachers to rank their first five topic selections and then to check three or four topics of lesser interest. This ranking system is illustrated in the sample checklist items in Figure 2. Another modification would involve use of a multipoint scale for ranking the importance or desirability of each item on the checklist. The sample checklist items in Figure 3 illustrate the multipoint scale format. Both of these modifications allow presenters to better determine which topics are likely to be best received by teachers.

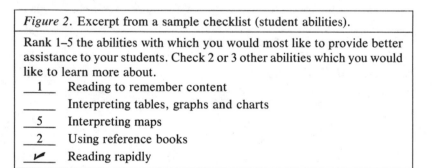

Figure 2. Excerpt from a sample checklist (student abilities).

Rank 1–5 the abilities with which you would most like to provide better assistance to your students. Check 2 or 3 other abilities which you would like to learn more about.

   1   Reading to remember content

          Interpreting tables, graphs and charts

   5   Interpreting maps

   2   Using reference books

  ✔   Reading rapidly

Somewhat more complicated variations on checklists include forced choices from sets of alternatives and dual scales. In the first case (Figure 4) two or three topics are included in a group and teachers select the one of greatest interest. A forced choice format works well as a means of selecting specific or critical topics once teachers have named a number of topics of interest. This format could be a second step in needs assessment or it could be used to select topics of continued interest once inservice sessions have begun.

In the second case (Figure 5) dual scales provide a means of determining perceptions of existing conditions concurrently with

Figure 3. Excerpts from a sample checklist (student abilities).				
What percentage of your students require assistance with				
	0–25%	26–50%	51–75%	76–100%
● using a dictionary ● using book parts ● evaluating arguments of authors				

Figure 4. Excerpts from a sample checklist (teacher practices).

Check one response to each item.
1. I am most interested in learning about:
    ___ assessing student reading levels
    ___ assessing readability levels of materials
    ___ identifying students' reading interests

2. I have a greater need to learn how to:
    ___ manage use of multilevel materials
    ___ manage small group learning

Figure 5. Excerpt from a sample checklist (teacher practices).

	How often do you now use these practices?			How helpful would these practices be to you?		
	Never	Sometimes	Often	Not at all	Somewhat	Very
Assessing student reading abilities						
Determining appropriateness of reading materials						
Preparing simplified reading materials						
Managing peer tutors						
Managing use of enrichment reading materials						

perceptions of needs. Teachers rank checklist items first on the degree to which they currently use them in content area instruction, and second on the degree to which they feel a need or desire to learn about them. Comparison of the two scales allows coordinators to select those topics which are of greatest need to teachers and to fit them into existing instructional practices.

Developing checklists or questionnaires to be used as needs assessment instruments requires much of the developer. Coordinators or committee members must have knowledge of content area reading and of the content area teachers who will use the instruments. Selection of items from the list of objectives in Chapter 3 should be made with particular teachers in mind and with a few general goals for the inservice series already determined. Differences in the needs of experienced and inexperienced teachers are discussed in Chapter 5 and should be considered when developing needs assessment instruments. Applications of reading may differ from one content area to another, as discussed in Chapter 3, and should also be considered as part of needs assessment. Needs assessment instruments should request demographic information so that coordinators and committees will know more about the population of teachers to be served.

Locating Existing Checklists and Questionnaires

The inservice coordinator or committee may decide to locate and use existing needs assessment instruments. These might be obtained from colleagues responsible for inservice programs, from state department of education representatives, from university professors, or from reading consultants. Any instrument obtained in this way should be scrutinized carefully, to be sure that it contains items related to content area reading and that its format is readable and will yield desired information. It is very likely that modifications will have to be made before an instrument is used with a particular group of teachers.

One extremely useful needs assessment instrument was developed by Allen and Chester (1978). Called "Assessment of Inservice Needs in Reading," it consists of three sections, each yielding information about aspects of content area reading. Section One asks for demographic information and provides good indications of teachers' previous exposure to content area reading and

Figure 6. Assessment of inservice needs in reading.

SECTION ONE
Please complete the following.

1. Present position (check most appropriate)
   a. Classroom teacher
   b. Administrator or supervisor
   c. Other. Explain.
2. Course or content area in which most teaching time is spent.
3. Grade with which you spend most of your teaching time.
4. Years of teaching experience.
5. Number of courses in: Developmental reading
   Corrective or remedial reading
6. Number of inservice programs in reading you have attended.
7. Please rate each of the following types of inservice on this scale

   1—preferred, 2—acceptable, 3—unacceptable.

   a. Lecture   _____   f. Teacher centers   _____
   b. Illustrated lecture _____   g. Visitations to other
   c. Demonstrations   _____   programs   _____
   d. Workshops   _____   h. Supervision from local reading
   e. Simulation activities _____   resources personnel   _____

8. On the following time-place matrix, please indicate your willingness to attend reading inservice programs. Fill in each square using this scale:
   1—almost always, 2—usually, 3—sometimes, 4—seldom, 5—never.

	Inservice in our school or neighboring school	Inservice anywhere within district or within 30 miles	Inservice outside district beyond 30 miles
After school	a	b	c
Saturdays	d	e	f
Professional days	g	h	i
Released time	j	k	l

Directions for Sections Two and Three
Step 1. Please rate each of the items in both Sections Two and Three as to how essential they are to your teaching. Use the scale shown and place your

responses in Column I (Important Practices).

1—essential   4—of little importance
2—important   5—of no importance
3—of moderate importance   6—lack of familiarity

Step 2. A variety of circumstances (e.g. lack of time, resources, training) may interfere with the use of skills and techniques which are considered important. What teachers consider important may not be what they can practice. To help us understand present classroom practices, please go through the items in both Sections Two and Three in terms of your present classroom practices and rate them on the frequency scale below. Place your responses in Column II (Present Practices).

A—almost always   D—rarely
B—often   E—never
C—sometimes   F—not applicable

Step 3. Finally, to indicate your priorities for Reading Inservice, please rate each item in both Sections Two and Three on a scale of 1–5 using the classifications below. Place your responses in Column III (Priority of Needs).

1—high priority   4—not very important
2—important   5—of no importance
3—of moderate importance

SECTION TWO. Techniques and Strategies	I Important Practices	II Present Practices	III Priority of Needs
1. Determination of the reading levels of material			
2. Identification and selection of appropriate instructional materials			
3. Identification and selection of appropriate supplementary materials			
4. Identification, use and interpretation of standardized tests			
5. Identification and use of informal techniques for assessing student potential			

	I Important Practices	II Present Practices	II Priority of Needs
6. Determination of students' reading interests and attitudes			
7. Determination of strategies for dealing with disabled readers			
8. Determination of strategies for dealing with superior students			
9. Determination of strategies for dealing with divergent interests and attitudes			
10. Provision for individualizing instruction (e.g., small groups)			
11. Determination and development of appropriate reading objectives			
12. Utilization of various questioning techniques			
13. Development of motivational strategies for the classroom			
14. Identification of strategies for teaching specific subject skills related to reading (e.g., graphs, maps, diagrams)			

SECTION THREE. Skill Development

1. Provision for vocabulary skills development			
2. Provision for comprehension skills development			
3. Provision for the development of critical reading			
4. Instruction in study skills			
5. Instruction in research and reference skills			
6. Provision for the development of rate and flexibility			
7. Provision for the development of word recognition skills			

their preferences regarding inservice participation. Section Two concerns teaching techniques and strategies which might be employed in content area classrooms. Section Three concerns seven areas of skill development in which teachers might provide instruction. Teachers are asked to rate each of the items in Sections Two and Three two times; first in terms of importance, second in terms of actual inclusion in instruction, and third in terms of priority for inservice.

The value of the Allen and Chester instrument comes from its content and its organization. Items clearly delineate strategies and skills which are of concern to content area teachers. The triple rating of items provides information which inservice coordinators and committees can use to develop objectives at all five levels discussed in Chapter 3.

Another type of instrument which could be used to provide useful needs assessment information is "A Scale to Measure Attitudes toward Teaching Reading in Content Classrooms" by Vaughan (1977).

The Vaughan survey provides indicators of general attitudes toward content area reading and also pinpoints particular topics toward which attitude changes are desirable. Nine of the survey's fifteen items are stated positively, and six are stated negatively. Allowing content area teachers to voice both positive and negative attitudes toward content reading gives them a sense that their feelings are important and gives coordinators and committees much useful information. For example, if teachers from several content areas react negatively to items dealing with vocabulary development, coordinators will know that this topic must be "sold" to the teachers in order for them to implement strategies learned in inservice. If teachers from a particular content area respond negatively to items dealing with the role of content teachers in reading instruction, presenters might schedule a special session to help those teachers better define their roles. Use of the survey at the end of the inservice program as well as at the beginning will provide vital evaluation information.

Group Discussion Processes

The use of checklists and questionnaires, no matter how well structured, may not yield all of the needs assessment information

Figure 7. A scale to measure attitudes toward teaching reading in content classrooms.

Directions: Read each item below. Use the scale to indicate your reactions to each item. Circle the number of the response that most closely describes your feelings about each item on the scale.

Strongly Disagree	Disagree	Tend to Disagree	Neutral	Tend to Agree	Agree	Strongly Agree	
1	2	3	4	5	6	7	
1	2	3	4	5	6	7	1. Content area teachers are obliged to help students improve their reading ability.
1	2	3	4	5	6	7	2. Technical vocabulary should be introduced to students in content classes before they meet those terms in a reading passage.
1	2	3	4	5	6	7	3. The primary responsibility of a content teacher should be to impart subject matter knowledge.
1	2	3	4	5	6	7	4. Few students can learn all they need to know about how to read in six years of schooling.
1	2	3	4	5	6	7	5. The sole responsibility for teaching students how to study should lie with reading teachers.
1	2	3	4	5	6	7	6. Knowing how to teach reading in content areas should be required for secondary teaching certification.
1	2	3	4	5	6	7	7. Only English teachers should be responsible for teaching reading in secondary schools.
1	2	3	4	5	6	7	8. Teachers who want to improve students' interest in reading should show them that they like to read.
1	2	3	4	5	6	7	9. Content teachers should teach content and leave reading instruction to reading teachers.
1	2	3	4	5	6	7	10. A content area teacher should be responsible for helping students think on an interpretive level as well as a literal level when they read.

Figure 7. (continued)

Strongly Disagree	Disagree	Tend to Disagree	Neutral	Tend to Agree	Agree	Strongly Agree	
1	2	3	4	5	6	7	11. Content area teachers should feel a greater responsibility to the content they teach than to any reading instruction they may be able to provide.
1	2	3	4	5	6	7	12. Content area teachers should help students learn to set purposes for reading.
1	2	3	4	5	6	7	13. Content area teachers should teach students how to read material in their content specialty.
1	2	3	4	5	6	7	14. Reading instruction in secondary schools is a waste of time.
1	2	3	4	5	6	7	15. Content area teachers should be familiar with theoretical concepts of the reading process.

Scoring the Scale

Nine of the scale items are stated positively and six are stated negatively. The negative items should be scored in reverse of the positive items, according to the table below.

Response	Response Value 7 6 5 4 3 2 1
Positive items: 1, 2, 4, 6, 8, 10, 12, 13, 15	7 6 5 4 3 2 1
Negative items: 3, 5, 7, 9, 11, 14	1 2 3 4 5 6 7

Siedow

Total scores are determined by summing the response values. These total scores can be interpreted according to the following criteria.

Interpretation Table

Range	Attitude
91 or higher	High
81–90	Above Average
71–80	Average
61–70	Below Average
60 or lower	Low

required for developing an inservice series. Even when coupled with motivational activities, completion of these paper and pencil tasks may not produce consensus among content area teachers. Because checklists and questionnaires are generally used before inservice actually begins, they may pick up only those needs which are most obvious or most immediately felt.

An alternative to the use of checklists and questionnaires is use of a group discussion process. Participants are involved in discussions and ratings until consensus is reached. A group discussion process usually begins with a very general listing step designed to elicit a large number of concerns and needs. In each of the succeeding steps the list is narrowed, usually through discussions, ranking, and tallying. Finally, a short list emerges, representing those concerns or needs which participants agree are most important or most critical. Wood, Thompson, and Russell (1981) describe the Nominal Group Process, a highly structured sequence of activities leading to consensus. The Nominal Group Process consists of individual listing, round robin presentation of individual items for inclusion on a master list, voting, discussion, and final noting steps. Interaction among participants is allowed only during the discussion.

When content area teachers are unfamiliar with the field of reading, or where considerable opposition to the proposed inservice series is anticipated, a group discussion process could be used to conduct needs assessment concurrently with the first few sessions of the series. The objectives, content, and presentation methods for these sessions would be concerned with acquainting participants with the terminology of content area reading, encouraging them to work together, and helping them develop a rationale for content area reading in their classrooms. As these activities progress, needs assessment activities could be conducted through discussion. Brainstorming about students' reading behaviors could produce a list of concerns as teachers become acquainted with reading terminology. Discussions and rankings of these concerns could be one group development activity that also results in a priority ranking of needs. If this much were accomplished in the first session, the second session could be devoted to development of a rationale for content area reading, modification of the priority rankings, and reaching consensus on topics for the next several sessions.

Two cautions should be raised in regard to this kind of needs assessment. It is a lengthy process, continuing through several inservice sessions, and it is loosely organized and may be mishandled. To extend a group discussion process through an inservice series requires the expertise of a well trained and highly organized coordinator who is willing to exercise strong leadership. When teachers are committed to inservice from the beginning, such a process may not be needed. But when considerable "group development" will be part of the inservice, the process may be helpful because it allows for interaction among content area teachers at each phase. With large faculty groups, checklists can be used as part of discussion processes, and voting can replace ranking to facilitate the process.

Standardized Test Results

Another source of information which can be used to assess the need for content area reading inservice is standardized test results. Most of the commonly used test batteries report scores on subtests and also provide some indicators of performance on abilities tested within subtests. While it is advisable not to assume too much from standardized test results, it is possible to use subtest scores as needs assessment. By compiling the indicators of performance on subtests, coordinators and committee members can identify areas of student need which in turn can be used to plan objectives for inservice sessions.

Many school districts regularly monitor student performance with test batteries. Scores and indicators of performance are reported by class or homeroom and copies of these reports should be readily available. Coordinators might collect class reports and compile lists of abilities in which large numbers of students need assistance. Teacher participants might be asked to bring class reports to needs assessment sessions. Here compilations could be made, and individual teachers could discuss their students' needs as compared to those of the total student population.

In school districts where testing is not done regularly, coordinators might want to administer the reading subtests of a standardized achievement test battery. Among the achievement batteries most commonly used are the Iowa Tests of Achievement and Proficiency, the California Achievement Tests, the Comprehensive Tests of Basic Skills, the Metropolitan Achievement Tests and the Sequential Tests of Educational Progress. Coordinators should examine the manuals and the report forms of these tests in order to select the one which reports abilities most closely resembling inservice objectives.

By themselves, standardized achievement test results might not provide enough information for inservice needs assessment. But used in connection with other activities discussed in this chapter, they can provide important information about student abilities to coordinators, committees, and participants.

In Conclusion

Needs assessment should be thorough, informed, and continuous, in order to ensure that modifications can be made to help make inservice receptive to changing and developing needs. When needs are assessed only at the beginning of inservice, participants have only limited knowledge about the subject and may not be able to correctly pinpoint needs. They may also find, through inservice experience, that what they perceived as a need is really a symptom masking an underlying need. Continuous or periodic needs assessment allows for modifications in inservice as changed needs become apparent.

The procedures and instruments used to conduct needs assessment will depend on individual situations. Where participants are known to coordinators and where they are receptive to inservice in content area reading, a simple ranked checklist or quickly conducted group process will result in consensus. But where participants are not committed to content area reading inservice, and/or where coordinators are unknown to teachers, greater effort will be required. In the latter case, it may be necessary to combine procedures, to begin with an introductory informative session, to follow this with a checklist and an attitude survey, and possibly to continue with a group process until a set of topics can be agreed upon. It may also be necessary to periodically review the needs assessment to be sure the inservice is on track and teachers feel they are receiving what they requested.

References

Allen, Sheilah M., & Robert D. Chester. "A Needs Assessment Instrument for Secondary Reading Inservice," *Journal of Reading*, 1978, *21*, 489-492.

Berman, Paul, & Milbrey Wallin McLaughlin. *Federal Programs Supporting Educational Change, volume 7: Implementing and Sustaining Innovations.* Santa Monica, California: Rand Corporation, 1978. (ED 159 289)

Johnson, Gladys Styles, & Carol Camp Yeakey. "Administrators' and Teachers' Preferences for Staff Development," *Planning and Changing*, 1977, *8*, 230-238.

Lawrence, Gordon. *Patterns of Effective Inservice Education: A State of the Art Summary of Research on Materials and Procedures for Changing Teacher Behaviors in Inservice Education.* Tallahassee: Florida State Department of Education, 1974. (ED 176 424)

Vaughan, Joseph L. Jr. "A Scale to Measure Attitudes toward Teaching Reading in Content Classrooms," *Journal of Reading*, 1977, *20*, 605-609.

Wood, Fred H., Steven R. Thompson, & Sister Frances Russell. "Designing Effective Staff Development Programs," in Betty Dillon-Peterson (Ed.), *Staff Development/Organization Development.* Alexandria, Virginia: Association for Supervision and Curriculum Development, 1981, 59-91.

Chapter Three

Formulating Objectives

David M. Memory

As Chapter 2 has emphasized, a key to the success of inservice programs in content area reading is the gathering and use of needs assessment data. The person or persons responsible for planning such a program should be aware of both student needs within a school or school district and needs and expressed wishes of teachers regarding content area reading. However, formulating objectives for an inservice education program is not simply a process of organizing the eagerly offered suggestions of students and teachers being served. Moreover, where suggestions are offered, they are usually varied, and the task of achieving the consensus discussed in Chapter 2 is rarely a simple and easy one. Leadership in content area reading is just that—leadership. Before the assessed needs and expressed wishes of students and teachers can be efficiently and accurately identified, the coordinator of an inservice program must have an idea of what those needs and wishes might be. For that information to be used effectively in planning such a program, the coordinator must have an understanding of how dissimilar and even conflicting needs and wishes can be accommodated in a schoolwide or districtwide program. This chapter will present a framework that can help school personnel provide the leadership needed in planning the objectives of inservice programs in content area reading.

Reading specialists who have led inservice programs in content area reading for some years often say that their biggest task is insuring a continuing impact of their efforts beyond the inservice sessions themselves. Content area teachers might show interest when teaching ideas are presented initially, but that is no guarantee of self-sustaining involvement by those teachers in the future. In fact, the more pessimistic observers of inservice education comment that content area reading programs often amount to little more than an isolated inservice session or two conducted reluctantly, attended unwillingly, and soon forgotten. To prevent this from happening and to produce the continuing effects that reading specialists seek, careful formulation of program objectives is essential.

The final goals of most content area reading programs usually involve student performance on standardized tests of content area knowledge and student grades based on teacher-constructed quizzes and tests and on papers, oral reports, and other student projects. Certainly these goals must be kept in mind in planning inservice sessions. However, objectives that focus on specific student learning are usually more helpful in the planning and implementation of inservice programs than are broad goals. Therefore, the discussion in this chapter will be restricted to more specific objectives. The final goals related to course grades and to performance on standardized tests of content area knowledge will be considered in Chapter 6 on evaluation.

The more specific objectives of inservice programs in content area reading can be classified into five levels, each of which is important if self-sustaining involvement by teachers is to be achieved. Those five levels and sample objectives follow:

1. *Teacher Beliefs*. The teachers will recognize that it is important for students to be able to independently answer higher level written questions on selections read.
2. *Teacher Abilities*. The teachers will be able to ask questions in a sequence that prepares students for answering higher level questions during class discussions.
3. *Teacher Practices*. The teachers will ask questions in a sequence that prepares students for answering higher level questions during class discussions.
4. *Student Behaviors*. Following preparatory questioning, the students will answer higher level questions during class discussions.
5. *Student Learnings*. Students will be able to independently answer higher level written questions on selections read.

Relationships among the Levels of Objectives

The ultimate specific objectives of inservice programs in content area reading—that is, the highest level of objectives—are the skills and knowledge that students are expected to learn as a result of those programs. If an inservice program is to lead to the self-sustaining involvement of teachers, then objectives at this level must be selected carefully. Some potential objectives related to student learnings are simply not realistic goals for any content area teachers, some are realistic only for teachers in certain fields, and some are not deserving of the time and effort of any content area teachers. Part of an inservice coordinator's or committee's job is to provide leadership and guidance in identifying the student learnings that can reasonably and wisely be set as objectives of a content area reading program. These desired student learnings will then partially determine objectives at the four levels.

It would be ideal if these student learnings could be observed soon after teachers have started working to produce them, but many of the skills and much of the knowledge that are the ultimate specific objectives of content area reading programs are not learned quickly and easily. Therefore, other evidence is often needed to convince teachers that their efforts are paying off. If such evidence is not seen, self-sustaining involvement of teachers in a content area reading program is rarely achieved. The most persuasive demonstration that results are coming is usually observed in the classroom behaviors of students. For instance, in the example given in the list of objectives above, teachers would be more confident that students are developing the ability to independently answer higher level written questions on selections read if they see that, following preparatory questioning, the students are answering higher level questions better during class discussions. Therefore, when formulating objectives for an inservice program, the coordinator or committee should be constantly thinking of student behaviors that can reasonably be interpreted as early signals that the ultimate specific objectives of the program are being achieved.

But experienced educators know that desired student behaviors rarely appear spontaneously; instructional practices of teachers usually have to produce, or at least induce, those behaviors. Hence, the next lower level of objectives that inservice coordinators must consider involves the teacher practices that will likely lead to the desired student behaviors and student learnings. Again the expertise of reading specialists is needed in formulating objectives at this level. In Chapter 4 we will consider in greater depth the criteria that should be used in identifying teacher practices which are worthy objectives of inservice programs in content area reading. In general, there are two main criteria. The teacher practices selected should: 1) have the potential for producing the desired student behaviors and learnings, and 2) stand a chance of actually being put to use. The professional experience and knowledge of reading specialists and data gathered through needs assessment are probably the best bases for determining which teacher practices meet those two criteria.

Experienced coordinators of inservice education might argue that teacher practices are the main hurdle in the implementation of any program intended to lead to more and better learning by students. They would contend that if those practices are chosen well, then the expected student behaviors and student learnings will follow. Hopefully the preceding paragraphs have demonstrated the importance of formulating carefully the objectives at the levels of student behaviors and student learnings. However, there is some truth to the view that teacher practices are the primary challenge for inservice coordinators. For that reason, the objectives of an inservice program must be designed to help insure that those practices will actually be put to use. Before instructional practices are likely to be implemented in classrooms, teachers have to feel confident about their abilities to use those practices successfully. Therefore, the next lower level of inservice program objectives should relate to teacher abilities. With some newly introduced teacher practices that are relatively simple or that differ very little from existing practices, it is easy for inservice coordinators to build teacher ability and, therefore, teacher confidence. With other practices, though, much inservice time has to be devoted to this level of objectives. The inservice coordinators must always keep this level in mind while planning programs.

Inservice coordinators must also bear in mind the truism that ability is very difficult to develop in learners who are not motivated to learn. This applies not only to children and adolescents but also to teachers participating in inservice programs. Before most teachers will focus their attention on activities designed to introduce and teach new instructional practices, they must believe that those practices can help them achieve their goals as teachers. Therefore, the first level of objectives for inservice programs in content area reading must involve teacher attitudes. If no efforts or only feeble efforts are made to generate positive, receptive attitudes, then objectives at the remaining four levels stand little chance of being achieved.

Developing Sets of Related Objectives

In the planning of an inservice program in content area reading, it is helpful to have objectives at the highest level—student learnings—in mind from the start so that they can guide the formulation of objectives at the other levels. However, these ultimate objectives will not necessarily be the first ones developed. The key task is for coordinators of inservice programs to consider objectives at all five levels before the planning process is completed.

There are three main sequences in which sets of related objectives might be formulated. One common sequence begins with objectives related to teacher practices. A group or an individual decides that a certain instructional practice is a desirable one and plans part of an inservice program to introduce and teach that practice. For those inservice efforts to be successful, the coordinator or committee leading such a program must also develop related objectives at the other four levels discussed. In the other two common sequences, planning begins either with desired student behaviors or desired student learnings; related objectives at the remaining four levels are then formulated. What follows is a description of the development of a set of related objectives around a teacher practice that has been identified as one major goal of an inservice program.

Imagine that the secondary reading committee of a certain school district has decided that a goal for the district reading program is to have students in every class be given fifteen minutes a week to read self-selected materials related to that course. In other words, teachers should have magazines and books available in their classrooms and should allow students to pick out articles and book sections to read during a weekly free reading period. Use of this instructional practice could then be set as an objective of an inservice program in content area reading. But if the persons planning such a program think no further than that objective, there is little chance that the objective will be achieved in any meaningful way.

Teachers can quite legitimately ask what such a practice would produce in the way of desirable student behaviors or student learnings. Will students given a chance to read in this way later discuss the topics of the course with greater enthusiasm and greater understanding? Will they borrow course related books from the school library and read them on their own time? In short, what are likely to be the benefits of free reading in terms of student behaviors? What will students learn ultimately as a result of such an instructional practice? Will they learn to enjoy reading magazines and books that they would have otherwise ignored? Will they perform better than they would have otherwise on standardized tests of vocabulary and comprehension? The program coordinators would need to be prepared to offer realistic appraisals of what might be expected in terms of student behaviors and student learnings if weekly free reading were used faithfully by teachers, and they should be prepared to defend the value of the practice for improving course grades, student attitudes toward the subject area, or student performance on standardized tests of content area knowledge. In other words, the coordinators should be able to discuss the potential contribution of this teacher practice to the attainment of the final goals of the content area reading program. Appraisals of the potential results of a teacher practice can help determine what procedures are used in evaluating the inservice program and should guide efforts to provide assistance following inservice sessions.

At the lower levels of the objectives hierarchy, the school personnel organizing efforts to get teachers to use free reading in content area classes must be concerned about teacher abilities and teacher attitudes. A goal of successful once-a-week free reading in every class is unlikely to be achieved if the teachers involved have little knowledge of how to collect and organize interesting reading materials in their teaching fields. Efforts to put that instructional practice to use will have mixed results if the teachers have no idea of how to generate student interest in the reading of self-selected materials and how to create incentives for using free reading time constructively. This means that the coordinator of an inservice program with weekly free reading as a program objective must identify the knowledge and skills that teachers will need in order to put that instructional practice into use successfully. Objectives relating to those abilities can be formulated to guide planning for inservice sessions and to help determine how those sessions will be evaluated. However, stopping at that point would preclude real success for such a program. To generate receptiveness among teachers initially, and to help insure self-sustaining involvement by them, the inservice coordinator or committee must consider the teachers' views. If certain student behaviors and student learnings have been determined to be realistic outcomes of weekly free reading, then it is important that teachers recognize those behaviors and learnings as worthy objectives of their instructional efforts. In other words, one part of planning an inservice program with weekly free reading as a goal is formulating objectives related to teacher attitudes toward that practice and toward potential results of its use. Those objectives, too, can guide planning for inservice sessions and will help determine how those sessions will be evaluated.

Inservice coordinators or committees may have difficulty specifying an objective at one or more levels for some teacher practices or student behaviors or learnings. Nevertheless, it is important to try to devise objectives at all levels. Formulating a complete set of objectives increases the ease of evaluating results and the chance of finding favorable ones. Positive results may be found clearly at one level even though they are not evident at other levels. If one or more levels of objectives related to an inservice topic are ignored, then reliable evidence of the success of inservice efforts might go unnoticed by the teachers and administrators whose continued cooperation and support are essential.

Identifying Deserving and Viable Objectives

As stated earlier, an important task for coordinators of inservice programs in content area reading is to provide guidance in the identification or formulation of program objectives that deserve the best efforts of students and school personnel and that stand a reasonable chance of being achieved. The primary bases for making decisions regarding program objectives must and should be the professional experience and knowledge of reading specialists and data gathered through needs assessment. The practitioners of inservice education in content area reading must rely primarily upon their own good judgment and upon the information that they gather from the students and teachers whom they serve. There is virtually nothing that can be said with finality that can provide detailed guidance when decisions are being made about program objectives. Nevertheless, two general suggestions deserve mention. Information related to those suggestions constitutes the remainder of this chapter.

One fact for inservice coordinators to consider when making decisions about program objectives is that teachers in different content fields have different views about student learnings, student behaviors, and teacher practices that might be the objectives of inservice programs. Therefore, inservice sessions for teachers in certain fields often will be different from sessions for teachers in other fields. Table 1, based on a study with content area teachers (Lipton & Liss, 1978), reflects that divergence of attitudes. These data are based on too limited a sample of teachers to be used uncritically in planning program objectives; however, they can alert inservice coordinators to differences in perspective which might exist and to which they should be sensitive.

Table 1*

Comparisons of Means for Rating of Importance of Specific Reading Skills

Skimming and Scanning	Means	Reading Aloud	Means
Special education	1.29[a]	Physical education	0.00[a]
Mathematics	1.50[a]	Science	1.29[ab]
Physical education	1.50[a]	Vocational arts	1.93[ab]
Fine arts	2.14[ab]	Fine arts	2.14[ab]
Foreign language	3.00[ab]	Mathematics	2.25[ab]
Vocational arts	3.21[ab]	Social studies	2.86[ab]
English	3.60[ab]	English	3.96[b]
Science	4.29[ab]	Special education	4.29[b]
Social science	4.29[b]	Foreign language	5.00[b]
Vocabulary Knowledge	Means	Read Quickly	Means
Physical education	3.38[a]	Physical education	1.13[a]
Special education	4.71[ab]	Special education	1.71[ab]
Social sciences	5.43[ab]	Mathematics	2.25[ab]
Mathematics	5.44[ab]	Fine arts	3.00[ab]
Art	5.57[ab]	Foreign language	3.00[ab]
Vocational arts	5.57[ab]	English	3.60[b]
Science	5.57[ab]	Vocational arts	3.64[b]
English	5.76[ab]	Social studies	3.86[b]
Foreign language	6.00[b]	Science	4.29[b]

* From Jack P. Lipton and Jody A. Liss. "Attitudes of Content Area Teachers toward Teaching Reading," *Reading Improvement, 15* (1978), 297-298.

Understanding Poetic, Subtle or Symbolic Writing	Means	Silent Reading	Means
Physical education	0.75[a]	Physical education	0.75[a]
Special education	0.86[a]	Fine arts	1.29[ab]
Vocational arts	1.29[ab]	Mathematics	1.31[ab]
Science	1.29[ab]	Science	2.14[ab]
Mathematics	1.50[ab]	Special education	2.57[abc]
Fine arts	1.71[ab]	Foreign language	3.50[abc]
Social studies	1.85[ab]	Vocational arts	3.64[bc]
Foreign language	2.00[ab]	Social studies	4.00[bc]
English	3.96[b]	English	5.04[c]

Note: Higher numbers refer to a rating of greater importance. Scale ranged from 0 to 6. Shared superscripts indicate means do not differ significantly.

The second suggestion for inservice coordinators is that sound decisions are likely to be made only if those decisions are based on accurate and relatively complete knowledge about student learnings, student behaviors, and teacher practices that are usually the initiating goals of inservice programs. Coordinators who do not know 1) how a certain reading skill can efficiently be learned in a content area classroom, 2) what student activities or behaviors are likely to contribute to the mastering of that skill, or 3) what teaching strategies can lead to those student behaviors, can provide little worthwhile guidance in formulating program objectives related to that reading skill. A short chapter cannot begin to provide the specific knowledge of this type needed to formulate objectives. Nevertheless, we have attempted to compile a bibliography of resources that can help inservice coordinators to gain such knowledge. That bibliography can be found at the end of this chapter. The listings of student abilities, teacher practices, and student behaviors (Figures 1, 2, and 3) around which the bibliography is structured are correlated with the tables that follow those listings (Tables 2 and 3). The term "student abilities" is used in the first listing rather than "student learnings" because only skills are included, not content knowledge. Obviously the learning of specific facts, concepts, and principles constitutes an important proportion of the objectives in most content area classes. However, reading and study skills are the student learnings upon which content area reading programs most commonly focus.

The listings of student abilities, teacher practices, and student behaviors were formulated through a selective review of recent methods texts in the various subject areas, through study of the content area reading textbooks now in print, and through this writer's reflection over his experiences conducting inservice sessions and teaching courses in content area reading. The listings are not assumed to be definitive. Nevertheless, some classification and labeling of potential objectives for content area reading programs are necessary to facilitate the presentation of ideas. These listings are intended to organize and clarify the presentation of important information in this chapter.

As discussed earlier, there should be five levels of objectives related to any topic selected for a content area reading program. With most inservice committees, initial discussions about a topic begin with only one level and often remain focused on that level for some time. The topics dealt with in the listings are presented at the level at which they are most likely to be considered initially by inservice coordinators. For example, an ultimate specific objective of a content area reading program might be that students learn how to learn new terms introduced in their classes. When the topic of word learning is considered by inservice committees, however, the initial focus is likely to be on what teachers can do to effectively teach new words, not on teaching strategies that can improve word learning abilities. Therefore, in the listings the topic of learning new words is dealt with primarily in the listing of teacher practices. There are, of course, specific techniques that can be used in analyzing the meanings and determining the pronunciations of new words, and content area teachers can contribute to the learning of those skills. Since those structural analysis and phonic skills are assumed to be usable independently by students, they are dealt with in the listing of student abilities. However, most important content area words should be taught; students should not just be left to figure them out. Hence, most of the bibliography entries related to word learning are found in the listing of teacher practices.

The user of these listings should recognize that doing assigned reading and doing voluntary reading are not assumed to be the only student reading and study behaviors that teachers are likely to be concerned about. In addition, most teachers want students to actually use the types of skills included in the listing of student abilities. Simply knowing how to perform those skills is not enough; students must use them in their work if the final goals of a content area reading program are to be achieved. Therefore, truly effective strategies for teaching such student abilities must also be designed to motivate their use. In contrast with these student abilities, doing assigned reading and doing voluntary reading are listed as student behaviors because the focus with them is on motivation, not ability.

Finally, many of the teacher practices included in the second listing could reasonably become objectives related to more than one student learning. For instance, for many senior high classes, managing the use of individualized lessons might be one of the teacher practice objectives related to using a dictionary, using book parts, and interpreting maps. The teaching or review of those skills would probably be done on an individual basis because only a few weaker students would need help in those areas. It is partly because of this wide applicability of certain teacher practices that they are included in that listing rather than being found as teaching strategies in the articles and book sections cited in the student abilities listing of the bibliography.

The articles and book sections included in the bibliography are by no means the only existing discussions of teaching strategies related to the potential program objectives included in the listings. In this writer's judgment, however, they are the best such discussions now available. That judgment is based on the potential effectiveness of the strategies, on their appropriateness for use in content area classes, and on the clarity with which the strategies are presented.

Figure 1. Student abilities.
_____

Analyzing the meanings of unfamiliar words and recognizing words in one's listening vocabulary by using context clues
Analyzing the meanings of unfamiliar words and recognizing words in one's listening vocabulary by using structural clues
Recognizing words in one's listening vocabulary by using phonic clues
Using a dictionary
Making inferences
Recognizing the main idea of a paragraph or longer selection
Taking advantage of the organizational structure of a reading selection

Reading to remember content
Using book parts
Interpreting graphs, tables, and charts
Interpreting maps
Using reference books
Conducting library research on a topic
Recording information from written sources
Reading to follow directions
Skimming and scanning for information
Reading rapidly
Evaluating the arguments of authors
Detecting deceptive techniques in writing
Reading orally
Translating verbal problems into mathematical language
Proofreading

Figure 2. Teacher practices.

Assessing student reading abilities
Assessing readability levels of materials
Determining appropriateness of specific reading materials for specific
    students
Teaching difficult concepts
Teaching words
Preparing students for reading assignments
Guiding students through reading assignments
Leading discussions about reading assignments
Managing the use of multilevel reading materials
Managing small group learning
Preparing simplified reading materials
Managing the use of individualized lessons
Managing the use of peer tutors
Identifying the reading interests of students
Managing the use of enrichment reading materials
Managing the use of magazines and newspapers as resources
Teaching content to and improving the reading of severely disabled readers

Figure 3. Student behaviors.

Doing assigned reading
Doing voluntary reading

Like the listings upon which they are based, Tables 1 and 2 are not presumed to be definitive. Cheek and Cheek's *Reading Instruction through Content Teaching (1983, pp. 47–49)* contains a table that reflects a noticeably different appraisal of the applicability of various reading and study skills in specific content area classes. Moreover, there is a strong argument for the view that virtually all reading and study skills are needed at some point in every subject area. Nevertheless, in most areas only certain of these skills are used regularly. Teachers usually have definite ideas about which student abilities and teacher practices are appropriate in their classes. These tables are this writer's attempt to identify which abilities and practices are likely to be viewed by teachers as appropriate in each of the main subject areas represented in middle and secondary schools. Making decisions about the appropriateness of potential objectives in specific areas is an important step in formulating program objectives that will stand a reasonable chance of being achieved. These tables can serve as aids in that decision making process.

For example, suppose that the science teachers in a school or district have asked for ideas about how to get students to follow lab directions carefully. The inservice coordinator could look at the table of student abilities and see that reading to follow directions is important not only in science but also in several other subject areas. With those areas in mind, the inservice coordinator could set up a session or sessions on that topic especially for the teachers of those subjects. Alternatively, an inservice coordinator or presenter might be told to plan a brief series of sessions for a specific group of teachers including art, communication, English, and music teachers. The coordinator or presenter could see from the table of student abilities that evaluating the arguments of authors (such as art, drama, book, and music reviews) might be considered an important student ability by those teachers. These tables should not be the only basis for deciding which objectives are appropriate; theoretically, needs assessment should be more dependable. As discussed earlier, inservice coordinators usually have to take the lead in suggesting possible topics for inservice programs, and ultimately have to make decisions about which objectives will guide the programs. The tables can at least contribute to those steps of the planning process.

Table 2
Student Abilities Commonly Needed in Specific Content Areas

	Art	Business	Communication	English	Foreign Languages	Health	Home Economics	Industrial Arts	Library Services	Mathematics	Music	Physical Education	Science	Social Studies
Context Clues	X	X	X	X	X	X	X	X		X	X	X	X	X
Structural Clues	X	X	X	X	X	X	X	X		X	X	X	X	X
Phonic Clues	X	X	X	X	X	X	X	X		X	X	X	X	X
Dictionary	X	X	X	X	X	X	X	X	X	X	X	X	X	X
Inferences	X	X	X	X	X	X	X	X		X	X	X	X	X
Main Idea	X	X	X	X	X	X	X	X		X	X	X	X	X
Organizational Structure						X							X	X
Remembering Content	X	X	X	X	X	X	X	X		X	X	X	X	X
Book Parts	X	X	X	X	X	X	X	X	X	X	X	X	X	X
Graphs, Tables, and Charts		X	X			X	X	X		X		X	X	X
Maps														X
Reference Books	X	X	X	X		X	X	X	X		X		X	X
Library	X	X	X	X		X	X	X	X		X		X	X
Recording Information	X	X	X	X		X	X	X	X		X		X	X
Directions	X	X				X	X	X		X	X	X	X	
Skimming and Scanning	X	X	X	X		X	X	X			X		X	X
Rapid Reading			X											
Evaluating Arguments	X		X	X							X			X
Deceptive Techniques		X		X		X								X
Oral Reading			X	X										
Verbal Problems		X						X		X			X	
Proofreading		X		X										

Table 3

Teacher Practices Useful in Specific Content Areas

	Art	Business	Communication	English	Foreign Languages	Health	Home Economics	Industrial Arts	Library Services	Mathematics	Music	Physical Education	Science	Social Studies
Assessing Abilities	X	X	X	X		X	X	X		X	X	X	X	X
Readability	X	X	X	X		X	X	X		X	X	X	X	X
Appropriateness of Materials	X	X	X	X	X	X	X	X		X	X	X	X	X
Teaching Concepts	X	X	X	X		X	X	X		X	X	X	X	X
Teaching Words	X	X	X	X	X	X	X	X		X	X	X	X	X
Preparation for Reading	X	X	X	X	X	X	X	X		X	X	X	X	X
Guiding Reading	X	X	X	X	X	X	X	X		X	X	X	X	X
Leading Discussion	X	X	X	X	X	X	X	X		X	X	X	X	X
Multilevel Materials		X		X		X	X						X	X
Small-Group Learning	X	X	X	X	X	X	X	X		X	X	X	X	X
Simplified Materials		X					X	X				X	X	
Individualized Instruction	X	X	X	X	X	X	X	X	X	X	X	X	X	X
Peer Tutors	X	X	X	X	X	X	X	X	X	X	X	X	X	X
Identifying Interests			X	X					X					
Enrichment Reading	X			X	X	X	X	X		X	X	X	X	X
Magazines and News-papers	X	X	X	X	X	X	X	X			X	X	X	X
Disabled Readers	X	X	X	X		X	X	X		X	X	X	X	X

Resources: A Bibliography of Sources on Improving Reading in Content Area Classes*

Articles and Book Sections

Context Clues

Cunningham, Patricia M. "Teaching Vocabulary in the Content Areas," NASSP *Bulletin*, 1979, *63*, 112-116. A series of steps

* When only the author names are given, a book is being referred to. Those books are listed at the end of this bibliography.

for guiding students to use context clues in determining the meanings of words in reading assignments.

Cunningham, Cunningham, & Arthur, pp. 25-28. A series of steps for guiding students to use context clues in determining the meanings of words in reading assignments.

Hill, pp. 286-288. Describes several strategies for teaching use of context clues. Includes sample exercises.

Moore, David W., & Sharon V. Arthur. "Possible Sentences," in Dishner, Bean, & Readence, pp. 138-143. A strategy for helping students learn to use context clues in determining the meanings of words.

Moore, Readence, & Rickelman, pp. 38-43. Two strategies for helping students learn to infer word meanings from context.

Roe, Stoodt, & Burns, pp. 53-57. Several techniques for helping students learn to use context clues in inferring the meanings of words.

Vacca, pp. 71-76. Discusses important types of context clues and how to teach their use through modeling.

Structural Clues

Burmeister, Lou E. "Vocabulary Development in Content Areas through the Use of Morphemes," *Journal of Reading*, 1976, *19*, 481-487. Several motivating activities for reinforcing knowledge of prefixes, roots, and suffixes.

Burmeister, pp. 144-160. A variety of activities for teaching and reinforcing knowledge of prefixes, roots, and suffixes.

Dale, E. L., & Jerry L. Milligan. "Techniques in Vocabulary Development," *Reading Improvement*, 1970, *7*, 3-7, 15. An approach for teaching structural analysis skills when introducing new words.

Dale, O'Rourke, & Bamman, pp. 92-162. Sample exercises for teaching prefixes, suffixes, and roots.

Forgan & Mangrum, pp. 237-248. A series of lessons for teaching students how to identify multisyllabic words, mainly by using structural clues.

Hill, pp. 280-285. Several strategies for teaching and reinforcing knowledge of prefixes, roots, and suffixes. Includes sample exercises.

Milligan, Jerry L., & Donald C. Orlich, "A Linguistic Approach to Learning Science Vocabulary," *Science Teacher*, 1981, *48*,

34-35. How to teach prefixes, roots, and suffixes while teaching new words.

Readence, Bean, & Baldwin, pp. 38-40. Two strategies for helping students learn to use knowledge of familiar words in analyzing the meanings of unfamiliar ones.

Roe, Stoodt, & Burns, pp. 57-62. Discusses teaching of prefixes, roots, and suffixes.

Thomas & Robinson, pp. 39-45. An approach for teaching students how to determine the pronunciation and meaning of a word, mainly by looking for familiar parts in the word.

Phonic Clues

Cunningham, Cunningham, & Arthur, pp. 268-276. An approach for helping students learn to identify words by comparing them to known words.

Cunningham, Patricia M. "Decoding Polysyllabic Words: An Alternative Strategy," *Journal of Reading*, 1978, *21*, 608-614. An approach for helping students learn to identify multisyllabic words by comparing them to known words.

Cunningham, Patricia M. "Decoding Demystified," in Dishner, Bean, & Readence, pp. 74-80. An approach for helping students learn to identify multisyllabic words by comparing them to known words.

Dictionary

Askov & Kamm, pp. 43-46. Discusses several ways to help students become better dictionary users.

Classroom dictionaries. Helpful explanations and activities for learning how to use a dictionary.

Dale, O'Rourke, & Bamman, pp. 276-300. Discusses skills needed in using a dictionary effectively and how to teach those skills. Includes sample teaching exercises.

Hill, pp. 288-293. Several strategies for teaching the use of word references. Includes sample exercises.

Jones, Don R. "The Dictionary: A Look at 'Look It Up,' " *Journal of Reading*, 1980, *23*, 309-312. Brief descriptions of varied techniques for improving dictionary skills.

Kennedy, Larry D. "The Teaching of Dictionary Skills in the Upper Grades," *Elementary English*, 1972, *49*, 71-73. An approach in which dictionary skills are learned through preparation of a slang dictionary. In content area classes, the current jargon of a field could be the focus of such a project.

Inferences

Crouse, Richard, & Denise Bassett. "Detective Stories: An Aid for Mathematics and Reading," *Mathematics Teacher*, 1975, *68*, 598-600. Describes use of minute mysteries to teach deductive reasoning.

Daines, pp. 161-163. A procedure for helping students learn to reach generalizations (that is, make complex inferences) based on reading selections.

Forgan & Mangrum, pp. 175-180. A direct approach for teaching question-answering strategies that involves explanation and modeling of the strategies by the teacher. Inferential and other types of questions could be dealt with using this approach.

Hafner, 1977, pp. 138-141. A strategy for helping students learn to draw conclusions.

Harker, W. John. "Teaching Comprehension: A Task Analysis Approach," *Journal of Reading*, 1973, *16*, 379-382. Also in Harker, pp. 66-69. An approach in which the teacher first analyzes the steps used in reaching the answer to a certain question and then asks questions that lead students through those steps. Inferential and other types of questions could be dealt with using this approach.

Herber, Harold L., & Joan B. Nelson. "Questioning Is Not the Answer," *Journal of Reading*, 1975, *18*, 512-517. Also in Dishner, Bean, & Readence, pp. 80-85 and Harker, pp. 48-54. An approach in which the primary task for students is to provide evidence supporting the answers they choose or give. Inferential and other types of questions could be used in this way.

Reid, Ethna R. "Comprehension Skills Can Be Taught," *Educational Leadership*, 1981, *38*, 455-457. An approach involving teacher modeling of the comprehension skill being taught. Making inferences, as well as other comprehension skills, could be dealt with using this approach.

Main Idea

Arnold, Martha Thompson. "Teaching Theme, Thesis, Topic Sentences, and Clinchers as Related Concepts," *Journal of Reading*, 1981, *24*, 373-376. Discusses how to teach understanding of main idea concepts used in content area instruction.

Baumann, James F. "A Generic Comprehension Instructional Strategy," *Reading World*, 1983, *22*, 284-294. An approach for teaching comprehension skills directly, which could be used with recognizing main ideas and other comprehension skills.

Brunner & Campbell, pp. 112-120. A variety of activities and exercises designed to develop the ability to get the main idea of a selection.

Donlan, Dan. "Locating Main Ideas in History Textbooks," *Journal of Reading*, 1980, *24*, 135-140. Describes a three-stage teaching approach emphasizing identification of subordinate/ superior relationships.

Jolly, Hayden B., Jr. "Determining Main Ideas: A Basic Study Skill," in Hafner, 1974, pp. 162-172. Techniques for teaching main idea skills.

Karlin, pp. 209-218. A variety of exercises intended for teaching skills used in getting the main ideas of paragraphs and longer selections.

Moore, David W., & John E. Readence. "Processing Main Ideas through Parallel Lesson Transfer," *Journal of Reading*, 1980, *23*, 589-593. An approach that moves from picture reading to listening to oral reading to silent reading.

Putnam, Lillian R. "Don't Tell Them To Do It . . . Show Them How," *Journal of Reading*, 1974, *18*, 41-43. Also in Harker, pp. 70-72. A procedure for teaching recognition of the main idea that moves from easy tasks to more difficult tasks.

Organizational Structure

Brunner & Campbell, pp. 141-147. How to help students learn to recognize the common types of organizational patterns and learn to use that knowledge in understanding selections.

Cheek & Cheek, pp. 207-218, 222-224. How to teach recognition of various types of organizational patterns and how to use special reading guides to help students understand and remember information presented in those patterns.

Devine, pp. 229-237. Discussion of the common types of organizational patterns and guidelines for teaching understanding of those patterns.

Herber, 1978, pp. 84-97. Preparation of written guides to help students take advantage of organizational patterns in reading assignments. Includes several sample guides.

Niles, Olive. "Organization Perceived," in Herber, 1965, pp. 57-76. Describes an approach for teaching perception of the organization of factual materials.

Olson, Mary W., & Bonnie Longnion. "Pattern Guides: A Workable Alternative for Content Teachers," *Journal of Reading*, 1982, *25*, 736-741. Using study guides to help students take advantage of the organizational structure of selections as an aid in understanding and learning information in textbooks. Includes sample formats.

Readence, Bean, & Baldwin, pp. 45-49. Importance of organizational patterns; several approaches for helping students learn to recognize those patterns.

Vacca, pp. 145-152. How to prepare and use reading guides designed to help students take advantage of organizational patterns.

Remembering Content

Aukerman, pp. 47-61. Describes a technique for surveying a chapter before reading it and discusses how to teach the technique.

Edwards, Peter. "Panorama: A Study Technique," *Journal of Reading*, 1973, *17*, 132-135. The PANORAMA study approach.

Forgan & Mangrum, pp. 198-210. The SQ3R and PQRST study strategies and how to teach them.

Manzo, Anthony V. "Three 'Universal' Strategies in Content Area Reading and Languaging," *Journal of Reading*, 1980, *24*, 146-149. Also in Dishner, Bean, & Readence, pp. 168-171. Descriptions of three strategies, including the Question-Only Strategy that can be used to encourage students to ask questions when reading.

Memory, David M., & David W. Moore. "Three Time Honored Approaches to Study: Relating the New to the Known," in Dishner, Bean, & Readence, pp. 216-223. How three types of information—principles, organization, simple association— can be used in remembering content and how their use can be taught.

Ortiz, Rose Katz. "Using Questioning as a Tool in Reading," *Journal of Reading*, 1977, *21*, 109-114. Strategies for getting students to ask questions as they read.

Robinson, Francis P. "Study Skills for Superior Students in Secondary Schools," *Reading Teacher*, 1961, *15*, 29-33, 37. Also in Hafner, 1974, pp. 185-191. The SQ3R study method.

Roe, Stoodt, & Burns, pp. 106-111. The SQ3R, EVOKER, REAP, and PANORAMA study techniques and a brief discussion of how to teach them.

Singer, Harry. "Active Comprehension: From Answering to Asking Questions," *Reading Teacher*, 1978, *31*, 901-908. How to get students to ask questions when reading.

Smith, Smith, & Mikulecky, pp. 252-258. Description of the PARS study technique.

Thomas & Robinson, pp. 161-188. Description of the PQRST study technique and how to teach it.

Tierney, Readence, & Dishner, pp. 45-53. Russell Stauffer's Directed Reading-Thinking Activity, designed to make students active thinkers as they read.

Tierney, Readence, & Dishner, pp. 86-93. Description of the SQ3R study strategy and the survey technique recommended by Aukerman.

Vacca, pp. 165-171. Russell Stauffer's Directed Reading-Thinking Activity, designed to make students active thinkers as they read.

Book Parts

Askov & Kamm, pp. 25-32. Sample activities for teaching the use of book parts.

Brunner & Campbell, pp. 53-71. How to teach use of the table of contents, index, glossary, appendices, and typographical features of a book.

Jewett, Arno. "Using Book Parts," in Herber, 1965, pp. 32-41. How to teach the use of book parts.

Kealey, Robert J. "Helping Students Read the Content Area Textbook," *Reading Improvement*, 1980, *17*, 36-39. How to teach use of the parts and features of a textbook.

Readence, Bean, & Baldwin, pp. 65-70. How to use a text preview to introduce a textbook to a group of students. Lists a set of questions to include in such an activity.

Graphs, Tables, and Charts

Askov & Kamm, pp. 94-122. How to teach the interpretation of graphs, tables, and charts. Includes sample exercises.

Brunner & Campbell, pp. 77-80. How to teach the interpretation of graphs.

Fry, Edward. "Graphical Literacy," *Journal of Reading*, 1981, *24*, 383-390. Various types of graphic aids. Includes general guidelines for teaching the reading and writing of different types of graphs.

Nibbelink, William. "Graphing for Any Grade," *Arithmetic Teacher*, 1982, *30*, 28-31. Step-by-step approach for teaching the construction and reading of graphs.

Roe, Stoodt, & Burns, pp. 133-140. How to teach the interpretation of graphs, tables, and charts.

Slaughter, Judith Pollard, "The Graph Examined," *Arithmetic Teacher*, 1983, *30*, 41-45. How to teach the reading of graphs.

Summers, Edward G., "Utilizing Visual Aids in Reading Materials for Effective Learning," in Herber, 1965, pp. 119-145. Discussion of charts, tables, and graphs and how to teach their interpretation.

Vacca, pp. 208-216. How to teach the interpretation of graphs, tables, and charts.

Maps

Askov & Kamm, pp. 125-186. How to teach the interpretation of maps. Includes sample exercises.

Brunner & Campbell, pp. 72-76. How to teach the interpretation of maps.

Ferguson, Jack. "Using Road Maps in the Junior High School," *Journal of Geography*, 1976, *75*, 570-574. A series of activities for teaching map reading.

Haas, Mary E. "Around the Map: A Game for Practicing Map Skills," *Journal of Geography*, 1980, *79*, 196-197. A game for practicing map reading skills.

McCollum, Dannel. "An Elementary Understanding of Maps," *Clearing House*, 1976, *49*, 332-334. Teaching a basic understanding of maps, beginning with construction of a map of the classroom and moving to use of maps of the vicinity.

Roe, Stoodt, & Burns, pp. 130-133. How to teach the interpretation of maps.

Summers, Edward G., "Utilizing Visual Aids in Reading Materials for Effective Learning," in Herber, 1965, pp. 102-119. Discussion of maps and how to teach their interpretation.

Reference Books

Askov & Kamm, pp. 46-48. How to teach use of reference materials.

Copeland, Amanda, & Lavelle Watkins. "Using Reference Materials," *Journal of Business Education*, 1979, *55*, 70-71. Discussion of the reference materials used by office workers, and several real-life activities for teaching use of those materials.

Mattleman, Marciene S., & Howard E. Blake. "Study Skills: Prescriptions for Survival," *Language Arts*, 1977, *54*, 925-927. Brief descriptions of real-life activities for teaching use of reference materials.

Sanacore, Joseph. "Locating Information," *Journal of Reading*, 1974, *18*, 231-233. An approach for teaching use of library reference books.

Library

Askov & Kamm, pp. 33-42. How to teach use of the card catalog and *Readers' Guide*.

Biggs, Mary. "A Proposal for Course-Related Library Instruction," *School Library Journal*, 1980, *26*, 34-37. How to help students learn library research skills during library projects.

Chesney, Bob. "In the Question Was the Answer: A Study of Trivia," *English Journal*, 1982, *71*, 41-42. The use of trivia questions to teach techniques of library research.

Devine, pp. 181-217. How to teach library research skills.

Hafner, 1977, pp. 169-173. How to teach use of the card catalog and *Readers' Guide*.

How to Use the Readers' Guide to Periodical Literature. An instructional booklet for students. Up to 50 copies available free from Marketing Services, H. W. Wilson, 950 University Avenue, Bronx, NY 10452.

Thomas & Robinson, pp. 127-147. How to teach library research skills. Includes a "Checklist of Locational Skills for Problem Solving and Topic Development."

Wilmer, Kathryn G. "Mystery at the Library," *School Library Journal*, 1982, *28*, 24-26. An activity for teaching library research skills that involves the solving of a mystery.

Recording Information

Brunner & Campbell, pp. 86-101. How to teach outlining and notetaking.

D'Angelo, Karen. "Précis Writing: Promoting Vocabulary Development and Comprehension," *Journal of Reading*, 1983, *26*, 534-539. A procedure for teaching students how to write summaries of selections read.

Karlin, pp. 219-225. Discussion of techniques for teaching outlining and summarizing. Includes sample exercises.

Palmatier, Robert A. "A Notetaking System for Learning," *Journal of Reading*, 1973, *17*, 36-39. A notetaking procedure that makes self-testing easy.

Roe, Stoodt, & Burns, pp. 111-118. Techniques for teaching outlining, summarizing, and notetaking.

Rubin, pp. 130-144. How to teach outlining, semantic mapping, summarizing, and notetaking.

Smith, Smith, & Mikulecky, pp. 262-267. Description of a procedure for teaching outlining.

Thomas & Robinson, pp. 188-195. Tips on taking notes and on helping students learn how to take notes.

Directions

Conroy, Michael T. "Reading and Following Printed Directions," *Industrial Education*, 1980, *69*, 24-28. Description of a lesson on following written directions.

Pearson, Herbert, & Ellen Lamar Thomas. "If Your Classes Have Trouble Reading Instructions. . ," *Industrial Education*, 1974, *63*, 22-23. Description of an approach in which industrial arts students are taught a set of guidelines on following directions.

Roe, Stoodt, & Burns, pp. 127-130. Techniques for helping students improve their ability to follow written directions.

Rubin, pp. 107-109. Techniques for helping students improve their ability to follow written directions.

Thomas & Robinson, pp. 315-321, 369-375, 378-383. Techniques for helping students learn to follow written directions in science, business, and home economics classes.

Skimming and Scanning

Memory, David M., & David W. Moore. "Selecting Sources in Library Research: An Activity in Skimming and Critical Reading," *Journal of Reading*, 1981, *24*, 469-474. Description of an activity used to improve skimming ability.

Rubin, pp. 109-114. How to teach skimming and scanning. Includes sample activities.

Schachter, Sumner W. "Developing Flexible Reading Habits," *Journal of Reading*, 1978, *22*, 149-152. Descriptions of activities for teaching skimming and scanning.

Thomas & Robinson, pp. 212-218. How to teach skimming and scanning.

Rapid Reading
Causey, Oscar S., & Joseph A. Fisher. "Transfer Techniques in Reading Laboratory Work," *Journal of Developmental Reading*, 1959, *2*, 3-10. Techniques for helping students transfer improvements in rate from machines to normal reading.
Daines, pp. 149-152. Descriptions of several activities for improving reading rates.
Fisher, Joseph A. "Transfer Techniques in Reading Improvement Courses," in Hafner, 1974, pp. 265-273.
Shelton, Nancy, & Shirley Warner. "Read Faster, Understand More," *Teacher*, 1974, *92*, 66, 68, 70-71. An approach for teaching rate improvement.
Thomas & Robinson, pp. 218-221. Techniques for teaching students to read rapidly.

Evaluating Arguments
Baldwin, R. Scott, & John E. Readence. "Critical Reading and Perceived Authority," *Journal of Reading*, 1979, *22*, 617-622. An approach to making students aware that they should be critical of what they read.
Hill, pp. 325-326. Helping students learn to assess the validity of the content of written materials.
Hoffman, James V. "The Intra-Act Procedure for Critical Reading," *Journal of Reading*, 1979, *22*, 605-608. Description of a structured procedure in which small groups of students discuss their views about a reading selection.
Mize, John M. "A Directed Strategy for Teaching Critical Reading and Decision Making," *Journal of Reading*, 1978, *22*, 144-148. Helping students develop the ability to analyze issues and arrive at their own reasoned perspectives.
Ross, Elinor Parry. "Checking the Source: An Essential Component of Critical Reading," *Journal of Reading*, 1981, *24*, 311-315. Techniques for teaching students to take into consideration the author's qualifications and bias, and the source of the selection when reading.
Sandberg, Kate. "Learning to Read History Actively," *Journal of Reading*, 1981, *25*, 158-160. An approach to reading history books involving evaluation of the main points presented.

Santeusanio, pp. 211-229. Three approaches for teaching evaluation of selections intended to persuade. Includes a sample direct teaching lesson, sample adjunct questions, and sample study guides.

Singer & Donlan, pp. 210-216. The inquiry approach to instruction in which students solve problems by careful examination, interpretation, and evaluation of evidence. Includes sample plans.

Thomas & Robinson, pp. 108-118. How to help students learn to evaluate the arguments of authors.

Deceptive Techniques

Armelino, Barbara Ann. "Developing Critical Skills through Media Analysis," *English Journal*, 1979, *68*, 56-58. Description of a unit for teaching the analysis of advertising.

Burmeister, pp. 268-272. The common propaganda techniques and methods for teaching students to be sensitive to them.

Kime, Robert E., & William T. Jarvis. "Consumer Health: A Difficult Teaching Area?" *School Health Review*, 1973, *4*, 6-9. Discussion of techniques for teaching the reading of advertisements.

Rader, William D. "Improving Critical Reading Through Consumer Education," *Social Education*, 1978, *42*, 18-20. How to improve the critical reading of advertisements.

Ross, Elinor Parry. "Travel Brochure Trips," *Teacher*, 1978, *95*, 60-63. Description of an activity for improving critical reading by using travel brochures.

Oral Reading

Niles, Doris. "Recorder Projects for High School Speech Classes," *Speech Teacher*, 1967, *16*, 219-220. Ways to use a tape recorder in improving oral reading and other oral communication skills.

Post, Robert M. "Ensemble Oral Interpretation," *Speech Teacher*, 1974, *23*, 151-155. How to use group oral reading of literary selections.

Romjue, Jane Murphy. "An Approach to Teaching Oral Reading to Eighth Graders," *Journal of Reading*, 1978, *22*, 221-223. A procedure in which students choose, prepare, and read a selection aloud to the class.

Smale, Michael. "Teaching Secondary Students about Reading to Children," *Journal of Reading*, 1982, *26*, 208-210. An approach for teaching secondary students how to read to children.

Tierney, Readence, & Dishner, pp. 128-138. Three techniques for improving oral reading—choral reading, radio reading, and paired reading.

Vacca, pp. 176-179. A method for improving oral reading—radio reading.

Widmann, Victor F. "Developing Oral Reading Ability in Teenagers through the Presentation of Children's Stories, *Journal of Reading*, 1978, *21*, 329-334. A program in which poor readers in junior high school read children's books to primary students.

Verbal Problems

Dahmus, Maurice E. "How to Teach Verbal Problems," *School Science and Mathematics*, 1970, *70*, 121-138. Description of a procedure in which all verbal information is put into mathematical form first.

Denmark, Tom. "Improving Students' Comprehension of Word Problems," *Mathematics Teacher*, 1983, *76*, 31-34. Four exercises for improving reading of word problems.

Forgan & Mangrum, pp. 210-217. The SQRQCQ approach for solving word problems, and how to teach it.

Henny, Maribeth. "Improving Mathematics Verbal Problem-Solving Ability through Reading Instruction," *Arithmetic Teacher*, 1971, *18*, 223-229. An approach for improving the ability to solve word problems.

Krulik, Stephen, & Jesse A. Rudnick. "Suggestions for Teaching Problem Solving—A Baker's Dozen," *School Science and Mathematics*, 1981, *81*, 37-41. Several activities for teaching the solving of word problems.

LeBlanc, John F. "Teaching Textbook Story Problems," *Arithmetic Teacher*, 1982, *29*, 52-54. How to teach an approach to solving word problems.

Maffei, Anthony. "Reading Analysis in Mathematics," *Journal of Reading*, 1973, *16*, 546-549. A variation of the PQ4R study method used for solving word problems.

Mettes, C.T.C.W., Pilot, A. Roossink, H. J., & H. Kramers-Pals. "Teaching and Learning Problem Solving in Science," *Jour-*

nal of Chemical Education, 1980, *57*, 882-885. An approach to teaching students how to solve problems in chemistry.

Pribnow, J. R. "Why Johnny Can't Read Word Problems," *School Science and Mathematics*, 1969, *69*, 591-598. An approach to solving word problems.

Richardson, Lloyd I. "The Role of Strategies for Teaching Pupils to Solve Verbal Problems," *Arithmetic Teacher*, 1975, *22*, 414-421. The step method and the translation method of problem solving, and research support for them.

Riley, James D., & Andrew B. Pachtman. "Reading Mathematical Word Problems: Telling Them What to Do Is Not Telling Them How to Do It," *Journal of Reading*, 1978, *21*, 531-534. The use of reading guides in teaching word problems; includes a sample guide.

Proofreading

Frankhouser, Pamela L. "Proofreading: That Old Bugaboo!" *Balance Sheet*, 1979, *60*, 315-316. An approach to teaching proofreading in which students exchange papers to check one another's work.

Howard, Janet M. "Teaching Proofreading for Information/Word Processing," *Business Education Forum*, 1981, *35*, 11-12. Brief descriptions of four proofreading methods and a discussion of how to teach proofreading.

Lundgren, Carol A. "Make Proofreading Fun!" *Balance Sheet*, 1980, *62*, 42-44. A game type technique for teaching proofreading.

Peterson, John C., & John Staples. "Declare War on Undetected Typing Errors," *Business Education World*, 1969, *49*, 9-10, 22-24. Common types of errors, effective ways to proofread, and guidelines for teaching proofreading.

Assessing Abilities

Ahrendt, Kenneth W., & Shirley S. Haselton. "Informal Skills Assessment for Individualized Instruction," *Journal of Reading*, 1973, *17*, 52-57. Also in Harker, pp. 2-8. The construction and use of an informal skills inventory. Includes a sample inventory intended to precede a unit in a business class.

Allington & Strange, pp. 84-88. Description of the assessment procedure recommended by Koenke.

Burmeister, pp. 47-55. The construction and use of an informal reading inventory modified for group use. Includes a sample inventory.

Carvell, Robert L. "Constructing Your Own Textbook Specific Study Skills Inventory," *Reading World*, 1980, *19*, 239-245. How to construct and administer a test to assess the ability to use the assigned textbook.

Dishner, Ernest K., & John E. Readence. "Getting Started: Using the Textbook Diagnostically," *Reading World*, 1977, *17*, 36-43, 45-49. How to use the cloze procedure, group informal reading inventories, and reading guides diagnostically.

Dupuis & Askov, pp. 52-61. How to construct and use a criterion-referenced group reading inventory. Includes a sample inventory.

Estes & Vaughan, pp. 68-93. The construction and use of a content informal reading inventory. Includes a sample inventory and interpretation of four hypothetical sets of results.

Forgan & Mangrum, pp. 106-120. How to construct and use reading skills tests. Includes sample tests.

Koenke, Karl. "Reading Evaluation by the High School Teacher: A Plan," *Journal of Reading*, 1972, *16*, 220, 222-225. A testing sequence emphasizing group tests intended to identify the appropriate reading materials and appropriate assistance for individual students.

Rakes, Thomas A. "A Group Instructional Inventory," *Journal of Reading*, 1975, *18*, 595-598. A group technique for both determining the suitability of a certain book for a certain student and for identifying skill strengths and weaknesses related to use of the book.

Rakes, Thomas A., & Lana McWilliams. "Assessing Reading Skills in the Content Areas," in Dishner, Bean, & Readence, pp. 119-126. The construction and use of a group reading inventory. Includes a sample inventory.

Roe, Stoodt, & Burns, pp. 285-298. The construction and use of a group reading inventory and skill inventories. Includes sample inventories.

Santeusanio, pp. 281-291. The construction and use of a group inventory. Includes a sample inventory.

Shepherd, pp. 153-163. The construction and use of group reading inventories. Includes sample inventories.

Tonjes & Zintz, pp. 82-86. Construction and use of a content informal reading inventory. Includes sample test items.

Vacca, pp. 284-299. Construction and use of content area reading inventories. Includes sample inventory items intended for use at the beginning of a course and ones to be used at the beginning of units of study.

Readability

Baldwin, R. Scott, & Rhonda K. Kaufman. "A Concurrent Validity Study of the Raygor Readability Estimate," *Journal of Reading*, 1979, *23*, 148-153. Discussion of the validity of the Raygor procedure. Includes the necessary instructions and graph.

Burmeister, pp. 32-38. Discussion of the Flesch and Fry procedures. Includes the necessary charts and graphs.

Fry, Edward. "Fry's Readability Graph: Clarifications, Validity, and Extension to Level 17," *Journal of Reading*, 1977, *21*, 242-252. Use and validity of the Fry Graph. Includes a reproducible copy of the graph.

McLaughlin, G. Harry. "SMOG Grading: A New Readability Formula," *Journal of Reading*, 1969, *12*, 639-646. Discussion of the validity and use of the SMOG Grading procedure.

Santeusanio, pp. 315-321. Use of the Fry, Raygor, and SMOG procedures. Includes necessary graphs.

Singer & Donlan, pp. 176-184. Discussion of the Flesch, Fry, and SEER procedures. Includes necessary charts and graphs.

Vacca, pp. 265-270. Use of the Fry, Raygor, and SMOG procedures. Includes necessary graphs.

Appropriateness of Materials

Allington & Strange, pp. 105-111. Discussion of the use of the cloze procedure.

Bormuth, John R. "The Cloze Readability Procedure," *Elementary English*, 1968, *45*, 429-436. Validity and use of the cloze procedure.

Burmeister, pp. 55-59. Use of the cloze technique, including a procedure for selecting a representative passage.

Rakes, Thomas A., & Lana McWilliams. "Assessing Reading Skills in the Content Areas," in Dishner, Bean, & Readence, pp. 126-130. Discusses use of the cloze test procedure.

Roe, Stoodt, & Burns, pp. 302-304. Use of the cloze test procedure.

Santeusanio, pp. 275-280. Construction and use of a cloze test.
Vacca, pp. 270-273. Use of the cloze procedure.

Teaching Concepts

Baldwin, R. Scott, Jeff C. Ford, & John E. Readence. "Teaching Word Connotations: An Alternative Strategy," *Reading World*, 1981, *21*, 103-108. An approach to helping students learn the distinctions among synonyms by using feature analysis.

Duffelmeyer, Frederick A., & Barbara Blakely Duffelmeyer. "Developing Vocabulary through Dramatization," *Journal of Reading*, 1979, *23*, 141-143. Use of dramatization to make word meanings vivid.

Dupuis, Mary M., & Sandra L. Snyder. "Develop Concepts through Vocabulary: A Strategy for Reading Specialists to Use with Content Teachers," *Journal of Reading*, 1983, *26*, 297-305. Several strategies for developing understanding of concepts and for building vocabulary.

Estes & Vaughan, pp. 167-174. How to construct and use reading guides designed to develop understanding of concepts. Includes several sample guides.

Grubaugh, Steven, & Roy Molesworth, Jr. "Teaching Vocabulary and Developing Concepts in Health," *Journal of Reading*, 1980, *23*, 420-423. An in-depth approach for teaching concepts that could be used in many subject areas.

Lewis, Jill Sweiger. "Directed Discovery Learning: Catalyst to Reading in the Content Areas," *Journal of Reading*, 1979, *22*, 714-719. A structured small group approach for helping students develop the key concepts needed in understanding reading assignments.

Readence, John E., & Lyndon W. Searfoss. "Teaching Strategies for Vocabulary Development," *English Journal*, 1980, *69*, 43-46. Also in Dishner, Bean, & Readence, pp. 148-152. Descriptions of two vocabulary building activities (List-Group-Label and Feature Analysis) that can be used in teaching difficult concepts.

Stieglitz, Ezra L., & Varda S. Stieglitz. "savor the Word to Reinforce Vocabulary in the Content Areas," *Journal of Reading*, 1981, *25*, 46-51. A teaching approach based on semantic feature analysis.

Thomas & Robinson, pp. 251-254. Brief descriptions of a variety of procedures for teaching complex concepts.

Vacca, pp. 152-156. How to construct and use reading guides designed to develop understanding of concepts. Includes several sample guides.

Teaching Words

Dale, O'Rourke, & Bamman, pp. 302-323. Sample exercises for reinforcing the learning of words.

Dupuis & Askov, pp. 175-180. Several activities for reinforcing the learning of word meanings. Includes sample exercises.

Forgan & Mangrum, pp. 131-143. General approaches and specific activities for teaching word meanings and reinforcing learning of those meanings.

Hafner, 1977, pp. 104-121. General approaches and specific techniques for teaching vocabulary and reinforcing word learning.

Hill, pp. 248-259. General approaches and specific techniques for teaching words.

Ignoffo, Matthew. "The Thread of Thought: Analogies as a Vocabulary Building Method," *Journal of Reading*, 1980, *23*, 519-521. The use of analogies for reinforcing the learning of word meanings.

Kaplan, Elaine M., & Anita Tuchman. "Vocabulary Strategies Belong in the Hands of Learners," *Journal of Reading*, 1980, *24*, 32-34. Five strategies intended to help students in content area classes become independent word learners.

Mangieri, John N., & Margaret Corboy. "Reinforcing Vocabulary in the Content Classroom: The Why and the How," in Dishner, Bean, & Readence, pp. 153-166. Sample exercises for reinforcing the learning of words.

Roe, Stoodt, & Burns, pp. 39-53. General approaches and specific techniques for teaching vocabulary and reinforcing word learning.

Thomas & Robinson, pp. 11-19, 36-39. General approaches for teaching vocabulary.

Tonjes & Zintz, pp. 156-165. Several techniques for teaching vocabulary and reinforcing word learning.

Vacca, pp. 230-238, 242-250. Exercises for reinforcing the learning of word meanings. Includes sample exercises.

Preparation for Reading

Gold, Patricia Cohen, & David Yellin. "Be the Focus: A Psychoeducational Technique for Use with Unmotivated Learners," *Journal of Reading*, 1982, *25*, 550-552. A strategy in which small group discussion helps create purposes for reading an assignment.

Langer, Judith A. "From Theory to Practice: A Prereading Plan," *Journal of Reading*, 1981, *25*, 152-156. A discussion strategy for assessing prior knowledge related to a topic to be read about.

Moore, Readence, & Rickelman, pp. 51-55. The construction and use of graphic organizers (diagrams representing the relationships among key concepts in a reading assignment).

Readence, Bean, & Baldwin, pp. 131-142. Several strategies for preparing students for a reading assignment.

Smith, Cyrus F., Jr. "Instructional Applications of Graphic Organizers," in Dishner, Readence, & Bean, pp. 143-147. The construction and use of graphic organizers (diagrams representing the relationships among the key concepts in a reading assignment). Includes sample organizer.

Stein, Harry. "The Visual Reading Guide," *Social Education*, 1978, *42*, 534-535. A procedure in which students work individually and then as a class to preview reading assignments by examining graphic aids in the assignment.

Thomas & Robinson, pp. 57-70. Ways to build knowledge and experience background, and ways to help students set purposes for reading an assignment.

Tierney, Readence, & Dishner, pp. 72-78. The construction and use of structured overviews (diagrams representing the relationships among key concepts).

Tonjes & Zintz, pp. 283-290. Construction and use of advance organizers (summaries of key ideas), and structured overviews (diagrams representing the relationships among key concepts). Includes sample materials.

Vacca, pp. 62-69. Construction and use of structured overviews (diagrams representing the relationships among key concepts). Includes sample overviews.

Guiding Reading

Brunner & Campbell, pp. 154-165. Construction and use of study guides. Includes sample guide.

Cunningham, Dick, & Scott L. Shablak. "Selective Reading Guide-O-Rama: The Content Area Teacher's Best Friend," *Journal of Reading*, 1975, *18*, 380-382. Construction and use of a study guide that helps students identify and learn the important information in a reading selection.

Hash, Ronald J., & Mollie Bailey. "A Classroom Strategy: Improving Social Studies Comprehension," *Social Education*, 1978, *42*, 24-26. How to construct and use study guides containing items on three cognitive levels.

Herber, pp. 55-65. The preparation and use of written guides to assist students in understanding reading assignments at three cognitive levels.

Herber, pp. 112-120, 125-126. The preparation and use of study guides intended to stimulate reasoning about reading selections. Includes sample guides.

Manzo, Anthony V. "The ReQuest Procedure," *Journal of Reading*, 1969, *13*, 123-126, 163. A procedure in which students and teacher take turns asking questions about a selection being read, allowing the teacher to model questioning behavior when reading.

Manzo, Anthony V. "Three 'Universal' Strategies in Content Area Reading and Languaging," *Journal of Reading*, 1980, *24*, 146-149. Also in Dishner, Bean, & Readence, pp. 168-171. Three strategies, including one in which the teacher periodically reads aloud a textbook selection and uses this time to answer questions and to provide guidance about reading the text.

McClain, Leslie J. "Study Guides: Potential Assets in Content Classrooms," *Journal of Reading*, 1981, *24*, 321-325. A type of study guide that deals with background knowledge, vocabulary, and comprehension of the reading selection.

Readence, Bean, & Baldwin, pp. 142-145. How to construct and use two types of study guides, including the Guide-O-Rama recommended by Cunningham & Shablak.

Tierney, Dishner, & Readence, pp. 11-18. The use of ReQuest, in which the teacher serves as a model of questioning behavior.

Tierney, Readence, & Dishner, pp. 69-72. Construction and use of a Guide-O-Rama—a set of questions and statements designed to help students understand and learn the key ideas in reading selections.

Vacca, pp. 120-137. Construction and use of study guides containing items on three cognitive levels. Includes sample guides.

Vacca, pp. 174-176. The use of ReQuest, in which the teacher serves as a model of questioning behavior.

Vacca, pp. 183-190. Construction and use of several types of study guides, including the Guide-O-Rama recommended by Cunningham & Shablak.

Leading Discussion

Cheek & Cheek, pp. 186-192. How to effectively lead discussion of reading selections.

Cunningham, James W. "How to Question Before, During, and After Reading," in Dishner, Bean, & Readence, pp. 198-200. Description of a procedure for formulating questions designed to help students learn the important ideas in a reading selection.

Davidson, Jane L. "The Group Mapping Activity for Instruction in Reading and Thinking," *Journal of Reading*, 1982, *26*, 52-56. A strategy for leading discussion about a reading selection.

Manzo, Anthony V. "Guided Reading Procedure," *Journal of Reading*, 1975, *18*, 287-291. A procedure in which students first recall everything they can about a selection read, then organize the recalled information with teacher assistance, and finally check their recall.

Readence, Bean, & Baldwin, pp. 145-151. Several approaches for leading discussion and guiding learning following the reading of an assignment.

Sanders, Norris M. *Classroom Questions. What Kinds?* New York: Harper & Row, 1966. Types of questions that can be used in class discussions and how to formulate those questions.

Singer & Donlan, pp. 111-123. Two approaches for leading discussion following the reading of an assignment. Includes an extended example of the Taba approach.

Tierney, Readence, & Dishner, pp. 32-35. Use of the Guided Reading Procedure developed by Manzo.

Vacca, pp. 171-174. Use of the Guided Reading Procedure developed by Manzo.

Multilevel Materials

Daugs, Donald R. "What Price Success? Multilevel Science," *Science Education*, 1971, *55*, 569-572. Also in Harker, pp. 24-28. Discussion of the use of multilevel texts in science.

Forgan & Mangrum, pp. 82-87. How to use differentiated reading assignments involving multilevel materials.

Glenn, Allen D., & Edith West. "Using the Textbook and Reading Materials More Effectively in the Social Studies Classroom," *Social Studies*, 1980, *71*, 163-167. Five options for accommodating students at varied reading levels, including the use of multilevel materials.

Roe, Stoodt, & Burns, pp. 348-350. The use of multilevel textbooks and multilevel supplementary readings.

Thomas, Ellen Lamar, & Philip Montag. "A Social Studies Department Talks Back," *Journal of Reading*, 1966, *10*, 22-28. Matching materials to the reading abilities of individual students. See also the chapters on comprehension and social studies in Thomas & Robinson's *Improving Reading in Every Class*.

Thomas & Robinson, pp. 76-84, 234-241. How to manage the use of multilevel reading materials.

Small Group Learning

Capuzzi, Dave. "Information Intermix," *Journal of Reading*, 1973, *16*, 453-458. A small group learning approach in which students teach one another.

Herber, pp. 200-208. How to use small groups in instruction in content area classes.

Readence, John E. & Ernest K. Dishner. "Alternatives to a Single Textbook Approach," in Dishner, Bean, & Readence, pp. 236-239. Includes descriptions of two approaches to small group instruction—Intermix and Jigsaw.

Singer & Donlan, pp. 123-130. How to form and use small groups in a classroom.

Slavin, Robert E. *Cooperative Learning: Student Teams*. Washington, D.C.: National Education Association, 1982. Descriptions of the major structured approaches to small group instruction, and the benefits of cooperative learning in student teams. Includes a bibliography of sources.

Simplified Materials

Conroy, Michael T. "Instructional Sheets for Students with Reading Difficulties," *Industrial Education*, 1979, *68*, 32-34. Discussion of how to prepare readable instruction sheets.

Craig, Linda C. "If It's Too Difficult for the Kids to Read—Rewrite It!" *Journal of Reading*, 1977, *21*, 212-214. How to rewrite material to the primary level.

Forgan & Mangrum, pp. 47-56. A procedure for lowering the readability level of written material, and how to write at particular readability levels.

Lamberg & Lamb, pp. 144-147. How to change the readability level of written material.

Luter, Robert R. "Readability: How to Improve Instruction," *School Shop*, 1977, *37*, 17-18. How to write readable instructional materials.

Walker, Charles Monroe. "High Frequency Word List for Grades 3 through 9," *Reading Teacher*, 1979, *32*, 803-812. Alphabetical and frequency listings of the 1000 most frequent words in the American Heritage Word Frequency Book.

Individualized Instruction

Aufsesser, Kathryn Summa. "Beyond the Ordinary: Learning Centers in Elementary Physical Education," *Journal of Physical Education and Recreation*, 1980, *51*, 36-38. How to use learning centers.

Blackburn, Jack E., & W. Conrad Powell. *One at a Time All at Once: The Creative Teacher's Guide to Individualized Instruction without Anarchy*. Santa Monica, California: Goodyear, 1976. How to develop and use learning centers, learning activity packages, and contracts.

Brunner & Campbell, pp. 165-173. How to construct and use learning centers.

Cochran, Cheryl. "Science Reading Kits," *Science and Children*, 1979, *17*, 12-13. An approach in which students create learning packets to be used by their classmates.

Dupuis & Askov, pp. 130-151. How to construct and use learning centers and learning activity packages. Includes sample materials.

Fleming, Natalie R. "Learning Centers in Elementary Art," *Art Teacher*, 1976, *6*, 10-12. The use of learning centers with specific suggestions for handling common problems.

Hainen, Judith. "Make Room for Learning Centers," *Music Educators Journal*, 1977, *63*, 46-49. The use of learning centers.

Kratzner, Roland R., & Nancy Mannies. "Building Responsibility and Reading Skills in the Social Studies Classroom," *Journal of Reading*, 1979, *22*, 501-505. Describes an approach in which students individually select topics, investigate them, and report their findings.

Krulik, Stephen. "Learning Packages for Mathematics Instruction—Some Considerations," *Mathematics Teacher*, 1974, *67*, 348-351. The preparation and use of learning activity packages.

Larkin, James M., & Jane J. White. "The Learning Center in the Social Studies Classroom," *Social Education*, 1974, *38*, 698-710. How to plan and use learning centers. Includes descriptions of two sample centers.

Ludden, Mary C. "Elementary Home Economics and Children's Literature," *Journal of Home Economics*, 1976, *68*, 17-21. Use of learning modules based on children's literature to teach home economics topics.

Morrow, Lesley Mandel. "Manipulative Learning Materials: Merging Reading Skills with Content Area Objectives," *Journal of Reading*, 1982, *25*, 448-453. The construction of learning centers. Includes three sample centers for content area classes.

Peotter, Jean. "Contracts," *Music Educators Journal*, 1975, *61*, 46-49. The use of an individual projects approach.

Petreshene, Susan S. *The Complete Guide to Learning Centers*. Palo Alto, California: Pendragon House, 1978. How to develop learning centers and manage their use.

Pruitt, B. E. "The Open Contract: A Program of Individualized Study," *Health Education*, 1975, *6*, 37-38. An approach in which individual students select topics and investigate them individually or in small groups.

Shear, Twyla, & Elizabeth Ray. "Home Economics Learning Packages," *Journal of Home Economics*, 1969, *61*, 768-770. How to prepare and use learning packages.

Solomon, Martha. "SIP's in the Speech Classroom," *Communication Education*, 1977, *26*, 270-273. How to construct and use self-instructional packets.

Steurer, Stephen J. "Learning Centers in the Secondary School," *Journal of Reading*, 1978, *22*, 134-139. How to construct and use learning centers. Includes a list of possible topics for centers in content area classes.

Telfer, Richard, & Don Moore. "Improving Reading in Individualized Science," *Science Teacher*, 1975, *42*, 22. An approach involving packets containing rewritten versions of key textbook passages, simplified explanations supplementing the textbook, and other teacher-constructed materials.

Tocci, Salvatore. "A Flexible, Individualized Approach to Instruction Using the BSCS *Yellow* Version, *"American Biology Teacher*, 1981, *43*, 148-151. An approach involving learning activity packages.

Ward, Patricia S., & E. Craig Williams. *Learning Packets: New Approach to Individualizing Instruction.* West Nyack, New York: Parker, 1976. How to develop and use learning packets.

Peer Tutors

Boraks, Nancy, & Amy Roseman Allen. "A Program to Enhance Peer Tutoring," *Reading Teacher*, 1977, *30*, 479-484. Training students to tutor their classmates. Includes a detailed listing of ten goals of the training.

Ehly, Stewart W., & Stephen C. Larsen. *Peer Tutoring for Individualized Instruction.* Boston: Allyn & Bacon, 1980. How to set up and manage a peer tutoring program within a classroom or school.

Larsen, Stephen C., & Stewart Ehly. "Peer Tutoring: An Aid to Individual Instruction," *Clearing House*, 1976, *49*, 273-277. How to organize and manage peer tutoring in a classroom.

Identifying Interests

Burmeister, pp. 69-79. Several techniques for identifying student interests and specific reading preferences.

Eberwein, Lowell. "What Do Book Choices Indicate?" *Journal of Reading*, 1973, *17*, 186-191. The use of an interest inventory composed of book titles and Dewey Decimal classifications. Includes the inventory.

Gentile, Lance M., & Merna McMillan. "Making Reading Real: Books and Self-Awareness," *Journal of Reading*, 1979, *22*, 629-633. A technique for getting information about student interests and concerns.

Karlin, pp. 271-273. The identification of reading interests, including a sample interest inventory.

Lamberg, Walter J. "Helping Reluctant Readers Help Themselves: Interest Inventories," *English Journal*, 1977, *66*, 40-44. Several types of interest inventories and how to use them. Includes sample inventories.

Lamberg & Lamb, pp. 336-341. Several types of interest inventories and how to use them. Includes sample inventories.

Rakes, Thomas A., & Lana McWilliams. "Assessing Reading Skills in the Content Areas," in Dishner, Bean, & Readence, pp. 117-119. Assessment of reading interests and a sample inventory for English classes.

Readence, Bean, & Baldwin, pp. 206-208. Assessment of reading interests and how to use that information. Includes two sample inventories.

Enrichment Reading

Allen, Irene Amilhat, & Kendall N. Starkweather. "Develop Reading Skills by Focusing on Change," *Man/Society/Technology*, 1971, *31*, 92-95. Discusses use of library research projects in industrial arts.

Baldwin, R. Scott. "When Was the Last Time You Bought a Textbook Just for Kicks?" in Dishner, Bean, & Readence, pp. 239-344. The use of trade books for supplementary reading.

Carroll, L. Patrick. "Those Pesky Book Reports," *Journal of Reading*, 1967, *10*, 468-472, 475. An approach to book reports that includes an objective test and options for topics to guide the writing of a brief essay.

Cline, Ruth K. J., & Bob L. Taylor. "Integrating Literature and 'Free Reading' into the Social Studies Program," *Social Education*, 1978, *42*, 27-31. The use of supplementary books in social studies classes.

Devan, Klein, & Murphy. "Priming: A Method to Equalize Differences between High and Low Achievement Students," *Journal of Reading*, 1975, *19*, 143-146. A procedure to equalize the reading demands on poor and good readers in an inquiry-based assignment.

Fraim, Emma Carville. "Book Reports: Tools for Thinking," *Journal of Reading*, 1973, *17*, 122-124. Several approaches to book reports that lead students to think about the books.

Nichols, James N. "Foiling Students Who'd Rather Fake It Than Read It or How to Get Students to Read and Report on Books," *Journal of Reading*, 1978, *22*, 245-247. Five formats designed to make book reporting purposeful and personally satisfying for the student.

Poole, Val. "Outside Reading and Book Reporting," *English Journal*, 1981, *70*, 37. A technique for motivating outside reading that involves guidelines for book reports written in class.

Sartain, Harry W. "Content Reading: They'll Like It," *Journal of Reading*, 1973, *17*, 47-51. How to use activity oriented projects to stimulate and guide reading beyond the textbook. Includes descriptions of sample projects.

Singer & Donlan, pp. 216-232. The concept technique and the project method: two approaches to instruction that involve reading outside an assigned textbook. Includes sample plans.

Smith, Cyrus F., Jr. " 'Read a Book in an Hour': Variations to Develop Composition and Comprehension Skills," *Journal of Reading*, 1979, *23*, 25-29. A technique in which each student reads a chapter of a book and presents it to the class, so that the whole book is discussed.

Stegall, Carrie. "Book Reports? Ugh!" *Language Arts*, 1975, *52*, 987-991. Using short tests in place of book reports.

Tonjes & Zintz, pp. 308-321. The use of collateral reading. Includes detailed information on compiling lists of reading materials to be used in this way.

Magazines and Newspapers

Allegrante, John P. "Well Read and Healthy," *Health Education*, 1975, *6*, 35-36. Discusses many ways the *New York Times* can serve as a resource for students and teachers in health classes.

Bibliography: Newspaper in Education Publications (4th ed.). Washington, D.C.: American Newspaper Publishers Association, 1982. Annotated bibliography of publications on the use of newspapers in the classroom. Available free from American Newspaper Publishers Association Foundation, Box 17407, Dulles International Airport, Washington, D.C. 20041.

Cimino, John, & Pascal de Caprariis. "Updating and Personalizing a High School Earth Science Program," *Journal of Geological Education*, 1976, *24*, 21-22. A program involving extensive use of magazine articles to keep the course up to date.

Cram, Yetta. "The Newspaper as Teaching Aid," *NASSP Bulletin*, 1967, *51*, 64-66. The use of a set of free newspapers for generating interest and building concepts in a consumer economics class.

Curriculum Innovations, Box 310, Highwood, Illinois 60040. Publisher of several magazines for use in middle and secondary school content area classes.

Scholastic, 904 Sylvan Avenue, Englewood Cliffs, New Jersey 07632. Publisher of several magazines for use in middle and secondary school content area classes.

Tiedt, Sidney W., & Iris M. Tiedt. "Teaching Current Events," *Social Studies*, 1967, *58*, pp. 112-114. Strategies for making the study of current events more interesting.

Disabled Readers

Dupuis & Askov, pp. 123-125. Using the language experience approach: An effective technique for improving reading while teaching content. Includes descriptions of possible uses of the approach in specific subject areas.

Esler, William K., & King Merritt, Jr. "Teaching Reading through Science Experience Stories," *School Science and Mathematics*, 1976, *76*, 203-206. An approach in which science activities lead to language experience stories.

Frankel, Jill Catherine. "Reading Skills through Social Studies Content and Student Involvement," *Journal of Reading*, 1974, *18*, 23-26. Also in Harker, pp. 81-85. Description of a seventh grade social studies class containing poor readers in which language experience, games, drama, and other nontraditional techniques were used.

Gold, Patricia Cohen. "The Directed Listening-Language Experience Approach," *Journal of Reading*, 1981, *25*, 138-141. Description of an approach in which students participate in the preparation of reading materials by listening to selections read by the teacher and then dictate summaries of what they have learned.

Meyer, Valerie. "Prime-O-Tec: Good News for Adult Disabled Readers," *Academic Therapy*, 1981, *17*, 215-220. An approach in which the student follows along in the book while listening to a tape of a selection. Designed primarily to improve reading, this method can also be used to communicate content.

Stine, Doris E. "Tenth Grade Content—Fourth Grade Reading Level," *Journal of Reading*, 1971, *14*, 559-561. Also in Hafner, 1974, pp. 462-464. Describes procedures used in a world cultures class containing poor readers.

Warren, Robert. "Helping Poor Readers in Secondary Science," *Science Teacher*, 1975, *42*, 55. How to prepare and use tapes of textbook chapters.

Motivating Assigned Reading

Anderson, Richard. "Consumer Education: An English Teacher's Case History," *Phi Delta Kappan*, 1979, *61*, 196-198. Describes the practice of giving brief daily quizzes over reading assignments.

Crouse, Richard. "Ripley's Believe It or Not—A Source of Motivational Incentives," *Mathematics Teacher*, 1974, *67*, 107-109. Use of interesting facts to introduce units and motivate reading of the textbook.

Fernald, Lott, & Lunstrum. "Relating Background to Comprehension through Word Association and Value Examination: A Case Study in Geography," *Social Education*, 1978, *42*, 21-23. An activity to motivate and prepare students to read an assignment.

Forgan & Mangram, pp. 266-274. Description of a general strategy for motivating students to do reading assignments.

Herber, pp. 181-187. Using a prediction activity to motivate students and prepare them to read a selection.

Lunstrum, John P. "Building Motivation through the Use of Controversy," *Journal of Reading*, 1981, *24*, 687-691. An activity that uses controversy to generate motivation for reading and discussion.

Macklin, Michael D. "Content Area Reading Is a Process for Finding Personal Meaning," *Journal of Reading*, 1978, *22*, 212-215. How to relate a reading assignment to the experiences and feelings of students.

Moore, Readence, & Rickelman, pp. 27-30. The use of Anticipation Guides to motivate interest in and thought about the topics of reading assignments.

Thomas & Robinson, pp. 53-57, 227-234, 264-268. Techniques for getting students interested in reading assignments.

Vacca, pp. 93-107. Several techniques for motivating interest in and thought about the topics of reading assignments. Includes sample materials.

Motivating Voluntary Reading

Brunner & Campbell, pp. 34-38. Techniques for motivating voluntary reading.

Bishop, David M. "Motivating Adolescent Readers via Starter Shelves in Content Area Classes," in A. Ciani (1981). Use of a classroom book collection to get students interested in reading voluntarily. Includes sources of information for selecting books for that purpose.

Chelton, Mary K. "Booktalking: You Can Do It," *School Library Journal*, 1976, *22*, 39-43. How to do booktalks to interest students in specific books.

Cornett, Charles. "Reading for Fun . . . in Science Class?" *Science Teacher*, 1975, *42*, 58-59. Description of a program of weekly free reading—an example of Sustained Silent Reading.

Cultural Information Service, 15 West 24 Street, New York, New York 10010. Periodical designed to help teachers take advantage of TV programs to enliven instruction.

Davis, Dorothy Voight. "Book Clubs in the Middle Grades," *Journal of Reading*, 1975, *19*, 150-153. The use of parent-led book discussion groups to make voluntary reading rewarding.

DeLooza, Diane E. "Students' Comment Boxes," *School Library Journal*, 1981, *27*, 34. Procedure for letting students know what other students have thought about books.

Erickson, Robert, & Ellen L. Thomas. "Art Class Book Collection Promotes Better Reading," *Journal of Reading*, 1968, *11*, 333-336. How to gather and maintain a collection of books in an art classroom.

Ganz, Paul, & Mary B. Theofield. "Suggestions for Starting SSR," *Journal of Reading*, 1974, *17*, 614-616. Suggestions for starting Sustained Silent Reading in a secondary class.

Gersten, Leon. "Getting Kids to Read," *English Journal*, 1981, *70*, 40-41. Step-by-step discussion of how to put on a book fair.

Haimowitz, Benjamin. "Motivating Reluctant Readers in Innercity Classes," *Journal of Reading*, 1977, *21*, 227-230. A reading teacher's techniques for motivating free reading.

Hill, pp. 343-345. A variety of strategies for stimulating voluntary reading.

Karlin, pp. 273-282. A variety of techniques for developing and extending reading interests.

Lamberg & Lamb, pp. 332-336, 341-342. How to develop motivation to read voluntarily.

Memory, David M. "Motivating Voluntary Reading in Content Area Classes," *Clearing House*, 1981, *54*, 313-316. A variety of techniques for motivating voluntary reading.

"On the Air for Reading," *Journal of Reading*, 1980, *23*, 486-487. Discussion of the efforts of TV networks to help educators

motivate student to read. Includes addresses to write for
information.

Prime Time School Television, 212 West Superior, Chicago, Illinois
60610. A periodical designed to help teachers take advantage
of television programs to enliven instruction.

Readence, Bean, & Baldwin, pp. 209-211. Discussion of the use of
Sustained Silent Reading.

Rubin, pp. 224-233. A variety of approaches for motivating voluntary reading.

Shepherd, pp. 134-139. Techniques for generating interest in reading
beyond required assignments.

Smith, Smith, & Mikulecky, pp. 86-99. Approaches for motivating
voluntary reading.

Thomas, Ellen L. "Books Are the Greatest," *Journal of Reading*,
1968, *12*, 119-124. A physical education teacher's strategies
for motivating reading.

Thomas & Robinson, pp. 403-409, 411-416. How to use art and
physical education instruction to motivate reading (many of
these ideas would apply in other subject areas).

Tierney, Readence, & Dishner, pp. 120-125. How to use Uninter-
rupted Sustained Silent Reading.

Witucke, Virginia. "The Book Talk: A Technique for Bringing
Together Children and Books," *Language Arts*, 1979, *56*,
413-421. How to use a book talk to generate interest in a
book.

Books Cited in the Bibliography

Allington, Richard, & Michael Strange. *Learning through Reading
in the Content Areas*. Lexington, Massachusetts: D.C.
Heath, 1980.

Askov, Eunice N., & Karlyn Kamm. *Study Skills in the Content
Areas*. Boston: Allyn & Bacon, 1982.

Aukerman, Robert C. *Reading in the Secondary School Classroom*.
New York: McGraw-Hill, 1972.

Brunner, Joseph F., & John J. Campbell. *Participating in Secondary Reading: A Practical Approach*. Englewood Cliffs, New
Jersey: Prentice-Hall, 1978.

Burmeister, Lou E. *Reading Strategies for Middle and Secondary
School Teachers* (2nd ed.). Reading, Massachusetts: Addison-Wesley, 1978.

Cheek, Earl H., Jr., & Martha Collins Cheek. *Reading Instruction through Content Teaching*. Columbus, Ohio: Charles E. Merrill, 1983.

Ciani, A. J., (Ed.). *Motivating Reluctant Readers*. Newark, Delaware: International Reading Association, 1981.

Cunningham, James W., Patricia M. Cunningham, & Sharon V. Arthur. *Middle and Secondary School Reading*. New York: Longman, 1981.

Daines, Delva. *Reading in the Content Areas*. Glenview, Illinois: Scott, Foresman, 1982.

Dale, Edgar, Joseph O'Rourke, & Henry A. Bamman. *Techniques of Teaching Vocabulary*. Palo Alto, California: Field Educational Publications, 1971.

Dishner, Ernest K., Thomas W. Bean, & John E. Readence (Eds.). *Reading in the Content Areas: Improving Classroom Instruction*. Dubuque, Iowa: Kendall/Hunt, 1981.

Devine, Thomas G. *Teaching Study Skills*. Boston: Allyn & Bacon, 1981.

Dupuis, Mary M., & Eunice N. Askov. *Content Area Reading: An Individualized Approach*. Englewood Cliffs, New Jersey: Prentice-Hall, 1982.

Estes, Thomas H., & Joseph L. Vaughan, Jr. *Reading and Learning in the Content Classroom*. Boston: Allyn & Bacon, 1978.

Forgan, Harry W., & Charles T. Mangrum II. *Teaching Content Area Reading Skills* (2nd ed.). Columbus, Ohio: Charles E. Merrill, 1981.

Hafner, Lawrence E. *Developmental Reading in Middle and Secondary Schools: Foundations, Strategies, and Skills for Teaching*. New York: Macmillan, 1977.

Hafner, Lawrence E. (Ed.). *Improving Reading in Middle and Secondary Schools*. New York: Macmillan, 1974.

Harker, W. John (Ed.). *Classroom Strategies for Secondary Reading*. Newark, Delaware: International Reading Association, 1977.

Herber, Harold L. (Ed.). *Developing Study Skills in Secondary Schools*. Newark, Delaware: International Reading Association, 1965.

Herber, Harold L. *Teaching Reading in Content Areas* (2nd ed.). Englewood Cliffs, New Jersey: Prentice-Hall, 1978.

Hill, Walter R. *Secondary School Reading: Process, Program, Procedure*. Boston: Allyn & Bacon, 1979.

Karlin, Robert, *Teaching Reading in High School* (3rd ed.). Indianapolis: Bobbs-Merrill, 1977.

Lamberg, Walter J., & Charles E. Lamb. *Reading Instruction in the Content Areas*. Chicago: Rand McNally, 1980.

Moore, David W., John E. Readence, & Robert J. Rickelman. *Prereading Activities for Content Area Reading and Learning*. Newark, Delaware: International Reading Association, 1982.

Readence, John E., Thomas W. Bean, & R. Scott Baldwin. *Content Area Reading: An Integrated Approach*. Dubuque, Iowa: Kendall/Hunt, 1981.

Roe, Betty D., Barbara D. Stoodt, & Paul C. Burns. *Secondary School Reading Instruction: The Content Areas* (2nd ed.). Boston: Houghton Mifflin, 1983.

Rubin, Dorothy. *Teaching Reading and Study Skills in Content Areas*. New York: Holt, Rinehart & Winston, 1983.

Santeusanio, Richard P. *A Practical Approach to Content Area Reading*. Reading, Massachusetts: Addison-Wesley, 1983.

Shepherd, David L. *Comprehensive High School Reading Methods* (3rd ed.). Columbus, Ohio: Charles E. Merrill, 1982.

Singer, Harry, & Dan Donlan. *Reading and Learning from Text*. Boston: Little, Brown, 1980.

Smith, Carl B., Sharon L. Smith, & Larry Mikulecky. *Teaching Reading in Secondary School Content Subjects: A Bookthinking Process*. New York: Holt, Rinehart & Winston, 1978.

Thomas, Ellen Lamar, & H. Alan Robinson. *Improving Reading in Every Class* (3rd ed.). Boston: Allyn & Bacon, 1982.

Tierney, Robert J., John E. Readence, & Ernest K. Dishner. *Reading Strategies and Practices*. Boston: Allyn & Bacon, 1980.

Tonjes, Marian J., & Miles V. Zintz. *Teaching Reading/Thinking/Study Skills in Content Classrooms*. Dubuque, Iowa: Wm. C. Brown, 1981.

Vacca, Richard T. *Content Area Reading*. Boston: Little, Brown, 1981.

Additional Book Sources

Culp, Mary Beth, & Sylvia Spann. *Me? Teach Reading? Activities for Secondary Content Area Teachers*. Santa Monica, California: Goodyear, 1979.

Dillner, Martha H., & Joanne P. Olson. *Personalizing Reading Instruction in Middle, Junior, and Senior High Schools* (2nd ed.). New York: Macmillan, 1982.

Smith, Carl B., & Peggy G. Elliott. *Reading Activities for Middle and Secondary Schools*. New York: Holt, Rinehart & Winston, 1979.

Thomas, Ellen D. *Reading Aids for Every Class*. Boston: Allyn & Bacon, 1980.

References

Cheek, Earl H., Jr., & Martha Collins Cheek. *Reading Instruction through Content Teaching*. Columbus, Ohio: Charles E. Merrill, 1983.

Lipton, Jack P., & Jody A. Liss. "Attitudes of Content Area Teachers toward Teaching Reading," *Reading Improvement*, 1978, *15*, 294-300.

Chapter Four

Planning Content

David M. Memory

In addition to formulating carefully the program objectives, coordinators of inservice education in content area reading must also use good judgment in planning the content of the inservice sessions and the sequence in which it will be presented. They must select wisely the assessment and teaching strategies to introduce and recommend in such programs, and must choose the most effective order in which to present the strategies. The first task, selection of content, will be facilitated if, as recommended in Chapter 3, the coordinators formulate worthy objectives that stand a reasonable chance of being achieved. However, planning efforts cannot remain at the relatively abstract level of program objectives. Inservice coordinators must also make detailed decisions about which instructional strategies to present during initial inservice sessions, and which ones to introduce later. The impression that initial sessions make on teachers and the success of the teachers' efforts in implementing recommended instructional strategies have a strong impact on teachers' cooperation in subsequent programs.

Selecting Content for Initial Sessions

There are at least four important criteria to use in choosing assessment and teaching strategies to introduce and recommend in the initial sessions of an inservice program. The instructional strategies to be introduced first should:
1. Be viewed as relevant and potentially effective in the classrooms of the teachers being served,
2. be easily learned by the teachers,

3. be easily blended into regular teaching practices, and
4. be likely to show desirable results quickly in classrooms. Keeping those criteria in mind can help insure the selection of instructional strategies that 1) will be accepted by inservice participants, 2) will be learned well enough to be used effectively, 3) will be put into practice, and 4) will produce results that lead teachers to continue use of the strategies. If these four things happen as a result of the initial sessions, future sessions are more likely to be well received, and the major goals of the entire inservice program will more likely be accomplished.

The first important characteristic of instructional strategies introduced initially is that they be viewed as relevant and potentially effective in the classrooms of the teachers being served. The planners of inservice sessions increase the chance of meeting this criterion if they are aware of some of the more typical views of teachers regarding widely recommended instructional strategies for improving reading in content area classes. For example, a study conducted with 33 secondary teachers and 18 vocational teachers who had been introduced to various assessment and teaching strategies (Dewitz, Henning & Patberg, 1982) revealed the range of attitudes shown in Table 1. In another study with 50 middle and secondary teachers (Criscuolo, Vacca, & LaVorgna, 1980), the varying attitudes reflected in Table 2 were found. Both of these sets of data make it clear that certain instructional strategies are likely to be well received more than others if introduced during initial inservice sessions.

But the views revealed in studies of heterogeneous groups of teachers are not the only kind of information that can be considered in selecting instructional strategies likely to be viewed as relevant and potentially effective. As stated in Chapter 3, teachers in different content fields have different views about student learnings, student behaviors, and teacher practices that might be worthy objectives of inservice programs in content area reading. When translated from abstract objectives into specific assessment and teaching strategies, these differences in views become even more apparent. Well designed needs assessment instruments can provide planners of inservice sessions with some of the information useful in accommodating the varying attitudes of teachers in different fields. However, some of the best guidance can come by examining the professional journals in the various teaching fields and by staying alert for articles written by content area specialists and teachers in

Table 1*
Secondary and Vocational Teachers' Assessment
of the Usefulness of Content Area Reading Strategies
on a 7-Point Scale (7 = Highest Utility, 1 = Least Utility)

	Secondary	Vocational
1. Assess the readability level of textbooks using Fry Formula and textbook evaluation checklists	5.55	5.47
2. Assess reading comprehension through the cloze procedure	5.32	5.15
3. Assess student reading ability through the use of informal tests	5.82	5.82
4. Assess interest by developing a student interest inventory	5.93	3.85
5. Use prereading motivational activities	6.45	5.60
6. Preteach difficult vocabulary	6.00	6.05
7. Teach contextual analysis	5.67	5.70
8. Teach structural analysis	5.40	5.69
9. Ask questions at all levels of cognition	6.63	5.98
10. Design reading guides	6.42	5.69
11. Use directed reading assignments	6.59	6.30
12. Establish reading skill centers	5.81	4.81
13. Group students for instruction	5.95	5.35
14. Teach flexibility techniques	5.39	5.12
15. Teach SQ3R and other study approaches	5.49	4.56
Mean	5.91	5.40

* From Peter A. Dewitz, Mary Jo Henning, and Judythe P. Patberg. "The Effects of Content Area Reading Instruction on Teacher Behavior," in Judythe P. Patberg (Ed.), *Reading in the Content Areas: Application of a Concept*. Toledo, Ohio: University of Toledo, 1982. Used by permission.

other journals. The teaching ideas described in such sources are more likely to be viewed as relevant and potentially effective than many of the suggestions found in reading methods textbooks and reading journals. A list of professional journals that occasionally contain useful articles related to reading improvement in content area classes is provided at the end of this chapter. Also provided is an annotated bibliography of articles selected from those sources because of the relevance or potential effectiveness of the instructional strategies described in the articles.

The second important characteristic of strategies introduced in initial inservice sessions is that they be ones that can be learned

Table 2*
Percentage of Responses Indicating the Degree of Sense for
Teaching Situations in Five Instructional Areas
Related to Reading

Instructional Area	Description	Makes Sense	Makes No Sense	Ambiva-lence	No Re-sponse
Evaluation	Informal Reading Inventory	.48	.24	.26	.02
	Student Placement	.48	.18	.34	.00
	Group Testing	.56	.14	.30	.00
	Readability Formulae	.70	.16	.10	.04
	Cloze Procedure	.30	.40	.28	.02
Decoding	Recognizing a Short Vowel Sound	.48	.24	.26	.02
	Recognizing a Vowel Diphthong	.50	.20	.30	.04
	Syllabication	.36	.34	.26	.04
Comprehension	Reading for Details	.64	.06	.28	.02
	Following Directions	.74	.12	.14	.00
	Sequence	.74	.08	.18	.00
	Anticipating Outcomes	.48	.14	.32	.06
	Distinguishing Fact from Opinion	.28	.30	.34	.08
	Creative Thinking	.62	.18	.16	.04
	Cause and Effect	.56	.18	.22	.04
	Main Idea	.52	.24	.20	.04
Reference & Study Skills	Dictionary Use	.60	.10	.28	.02
	SQ3R	.66	.14	.18	.02
	Using an Index	.72	.14	.12	.02
	Skimming and Scanning	.48	.28	.20	.04
	Using a Card Catalog	.60	.16	.20	.04
	Outlining	.68	.18	.14	.00
	Changing Boldface Print into Questions	.50	.14	.32	.04
	Reading Rate	.50	.28	.22	.00

Instructional Area	Description	Makes Sense	Makes No Sense	Ambiva- lence	No Re- sponse
Vocabulary	Root Words	.68	.16	.16	.00
	Prefixes	.74	.16	.10	.00
	Words in Context	.66	.20	.12	.02
	Etymology	.40	.34	.26	.00

* From Nicholas P. Criscuolo, Richard T. Vacca, and Joseph J. LaVorgna. "What Reading Strategies Make Sense to Content Area Teachers?" *Reading World, 19* (1980), 269-270. Used by permission of The College Reading Association and the authors.

easily. Of course, how easily an instructional strategy can be learned depends greatly on how well it is presented. Guidelines for selecting or designing effective methods of presentation are discussed in Chapter 5; we will restrict our discussion here to the issue of choosing strategies that are inherently easy to learn. Unfortunately, no simple procedures exist for distinguishing between strategies that can be learned only with great difficulty and ones that can be learned easily. Probably the best advice is to say that no single person should attempt to make that determination alone. Even if only one individual has the responsibility of planning the content of inservice sessions, he or she should seek out the assessments of other school personnel regarding the ease with which the strategies under consideration are likely to be learned. If an instructional strategy introduced in an initial session proves difficult to learn and, in fact, is not learned well by some participants, then there will be little enthusiasm for trying out that strategy in classrooms. Or it will be tried and it will fail. In either case, inservice presenters during future sessions will find it increasingly difficult to gain the attention and cooperation of participating teachers.

For example, one teaching strategy that is probably too difficult to consider introducing early in an inservice program is the use of modeling to teach inferencing ability. Teachers using this strategy are expected to explain step by step how they have gone through the process of making a certain inference. With simple inferences this instructional task is not difficult. However, with the more complex inferences that many students fail to make, teachers often are not truly aware of the steps they used in making the inferences. Even if they have a notion of an effective step-by-step process for making a certain inference, that specific process might not be one that most students can follow. Clues and reasoning paths for one person do not necessarily serve the same function for another person. In trying to use this teaching strategy after only brief training, not only is the teacher likely to be puzzled by how to proceed, but the students frequently will be confused by the guidance the hastily trained teacher tries to offer. If introduced in an initial inservice session, an instructional strategy as difficult to learn as this one can be expected to produce frustration sooner or later for the participating teachers, for their students, or for both.

The third criterion to consider in selecting the content of initial inservice sessions is that the recommended strategies be ones that can be blended easily into regular teaching practices. If teachers are doing a basically good job, it is no criticism to say that they do not wish to make major changes in the teaching practices in use. Teaching is difficult work, and tinkering with a successful formula can be unwise. Obviously, if new instructional strategies are to be used, then some changes are inevitable. However, in initial inservice sessions it is important for teachers to see that they can become even more successful without making major adjustments in their teaching procedures. Recommended instructional strategies that can be blended into the practices already in use are more likely to be well received by inservice participants and more likely to actually be tried out in their classrooms. If the strategies introduced in initial sessions are not given a chance to succeed in the classrooms of participating teachers, then future recommendations are even less likely to be accepted and put into practice.

The infrequency of major success stories in content area reading gives us no clear-cut guidelines for deciding which instructional strategies are likely to be put to use and which are not. Consequently, coordinators and presenters in inservice programs are forced to rely heavily on judgment in identifying strategies that can be blended into regular teaching practices. Many of the articles listed at the end of this chapter describe the actual blending of reading improvement strategies into common instructional procedures. Therefore, those articles can be helpful in planning the content of initial inservice sessions. In general, though, the most helpful source of advice for planners of such sessions is teachers in the content fields to be served, preferably teachers who are both perceptive in evaluating ideas and candid in expressing their evaluations.

The fourth criterion to remember when choosing the content of initial inservice sessions is that the suggested instructional strategies be ones that are likely to show desirable results quickly in classrooms. If inservice participants have accepted the recommendation of a presenter and have begun using a strategy intended to improve reading, those teachers certainly have the right to expect some payoff for their efforts. If they have been led to believe or allowed to assume that noticeable results will appear soon, the absence of such results can seriously dampen the prospects for the success of future inservice sessions. Experienced reading specialists know that dramatic improvements in the vocabulary and comprehension abilities of older students are rare, but content area teachers being asked to change the way they do their jobs deserve more than the tempered expectations of veteran reading specialists. When teachers are first asked to commit time and energy to a content area reading program, they should be introduced to instructional strategies that will indeed produce results they can see clearly and soon. As explained in Chapter 3, the first results may be student behaviors rather than student learnings. But in some way, the planners of initial inservice sessions should be able to say that the strategies they recommend can lead to observable and prompt results.

Again the articles listed at the end of this chapter can offer some guidance to inservice presenters and coordinators. Many of those articles describe strategies which their authors claim have produced the kinds of results that content area teachers seek. However, there are other good reading improvement strategies for which those articles do not provide documented support. Some of these strategies are presented convincingly in the articles and book sections cited in the bibliography in Chapter 3, and some are presented in the book sections listed in an additional bibliography at the end of this chapter. In the absence of persuasive written testimony, the professional experience and knowledge of the reading specialists involved in inservice programs are the best source of guidance for selecting instructional strategies that will show results quickly in classrooms.

Selecting Content for Later Sessions

Rarely can an entire series of inservice sessions on content area reading be planned ahead of time and be expected to unfold successfully on schedule. Frequently not as much is accomplished during initial sessions as was hoped, and some later sessions have to be used for further practice and refinement of the first instructional strategies introduced. In addition, the evaluation that follows initial sessions often reveals the need to redirect efforts away from the content that was tentatively planned for later sessions. Changes in the program in response to recognized needs are not only expected, but desirable. However, some types of instructional strategies should be reserved for later sessions, and changes in plans should not force that content into the initial sessions. The characteristics of assessment and teaching strategies that should be restricted to later inservice sessions deserve separate attention.

If the initial sessions of an inservice program have been planned and presented well, then some teachers will be interested in learning more ideas for improving the reading of their students. They would be eager to continue if there were an unlimited reserve of teaching strategies that are easily learned, easily blended into regular instructional practices, and that quickly show desirable results. But that is not the situation in content area reading. Some potentially effective strategies for improving reading take considerable time and effort to learn, some require extra time and effort and changes in routine if they are to be implemented in classrooms, and some do not produce results quickly. If strategies with any of these unappealing characteristics are to be recommended in inservice sessions, then there are other criteria to consider which differ from the four used in selecting the content of initial sessions. To convince teachers of the relevance and potential effectiveness of these less attractive instructional strategies, it is necessary to introduce such strategies in later sessions, not in the sessions that make the initial impression on teachers. The more demanding instructional strategies introduced in later sessions should be clearly seen 1) to capitalize on the strengths of already accepted strategies, and 2) to have the potential for helping solve pressing problems or for otherwise contributing significantly to student learning.

If an instructional strategy demands more of teachers and promises results less quickly, there is greater need to demonstrate the relevance and potential effectiveness of that strategy. One of the best ways to do that is to show teachers how such a strategy capitalizes on the strengths of other strategies that have already been learned, tested, and proven successful. For example, teachers may have been introduced to the idea of systematically teaching the key words used in textbook chapters. They may have learned how to define and explain words in simple terms and in ways that utilize the experiences and prior knowledge of students. And they may have learned to use new words in several sample sentences illustrating the contexts in which students are likely to hear or see the words used. If those teachers have observed that their teaching efforts have led to better student performance on tests, then they may be open to ideas about related, but more demanding, ways to help students learn vocabulary. For instance, they might be willing to try writing simplified glossaries to be used especially by less able readers as they study textbook chapters. Since the preparation of such glossaries would require time and careful thought, some teachers might be reluctant to consider their use. But if the teachers' initial efforts to upgrade their vocabulary instruction have been successful, they are more likely to be willing to try out a strategy that demands more of their time, effort, and thought. A key characteristic, therefore, of the more involved instructional strategies that might be introduced in later inservice sessions is that they clearly be seen to capitalize on the strengths of already accepted strategies.

Another criterion for selecting the content of later sessions involves the potential payoff of the recommended strategies. If an instructional strategy requires a substantial added commitment of teacher time, effort, and thought, then the inservice participants need to be able to feel that the commitment is likely to help solve pressing problems or otherwise contribute significantly to student learning. A major effort intended to accomplish little will probably be rejected. For example, the rewriting of a textbook to accommodate two or three students who have difficulty with the book in use is unlikely to be viewed as a reasonable strategy for improving reading in a content area classroom. Therefore, inservice coordinators should search long and hard for a more appealing strategy before deciding to recommend rewriting as a solution to the problem of a poor match between student ability and textbook difficulty.

On the other hand, the use of multilevel texts might be viewed as strategy worth trying for several reasons. Like a teacher-prepared simplified version of a textbook, an easy reading published text would be more understandable to less able readers than the on-level textbook. But unlike teacher prepared materials, easy-reading published texts usually have helpful study questions and other study aids built in that can contribute greatly to student learning. The use of one or more alternate textbooks for less able readers would likely expose those students to some ideas not found in the on-level text and would, therefore, make it easier for those students to make special contributions to class discussions. Equally important, too, would be the increased opportunities to discuss issues related to critical reading and critical thinking. Different textbooks usually express different viewpoints in at least some key areas, and students enjoy and profit from discussing the relative merits of such differing viewpoints. In general, if more demanding instructional strategies are considered for later inservice sessions, those strategies should be viewed as likely to produce major benefits at least equal to their costs in time, effort, and thought.

The articles cited in the bibliography that follows contain descriptions of many instructional strategies that can contribute significantly to student learning and to reading improvement in content area classes. Some of those strategies are demanding enough to be reserved for later sessions in inservice programs, but many have the characteristics that make them suitable for initial sessions. In selecting the articles to include in the bibliography and in choosing the book sections and booklets to recommend, this writer has kept in mind the criteria discussed in this chapter for selecting content for inservice programs. In fact, many of the articles are so persuasively written that they can serve to help convince teachers of the value of the strategies described. Nevertheless, users of this resource list and table must still exercise good judgment in deciding which teaching techniques to introduce and recommend in inservice programs.

Resources

Professional journals containing useful articles.

Art

      Art Education
      Art Teacher
      School Arts

Business
Balance Sheet
Business Education Forum
Business Education World
Journal of Business Education

Communication
Communication Education
English Journal
Language Arts

English
English Journal
Journal of Reading
Language Arts

Foreign Languages
Foreign Language Annals
Modern Language Journal

Health
Health Education

Home Economics
Forecast for Home Economics
Illinois Teacher of Home Economics
Journal of Home Economics

Industrial Arts
Industrial Education
Man/Society/Technology
School Shop
Vocational Education

Library Services
School Library Journal
Wilson Library Bulletin

Mathematics
Arithmetic Teacher
Mathematics Teacher
School Science and Mathematics

Music
    Choral Journal
    Instrumentalist
    Music Educators Journal

Physical Education
    Journal of Physical Education, Recreation, and Dance

Science
    American Biology Teacher
    Journal of Chemical Education
    Journal of Geological Education
    Physics Teacher
    School Science and Mathematics
    Science and Children
    Science Teacher

Social Studies
    Journal of Geography
    Social Education
    Social Studies

General
    Clearing House
    Educational Leadership
    High School Journal
    NASSP Bulletin

Journal Articles—Bibliography

Art

Cohen, Frances L. "Cover Story," *Teacher*, 1979, *96*, 94, 96, 98. Describes an activity in which children create book jackets for books they have read.

Corwin, Sylvia K. "Reading Improvement through Art: Success Story from the Big Apple," *School Arts*, 1977, *76*, 52-53. Update on one of the projects described by O'Brien.

Corwin, Sylvia K. "Art as a Tool for Learning," *School Arts*, 1978, *77*, 34-35, 51. Update on the project described in the earlier Corwin article.

Erickson, Robert, & Ellen L. Thomas. "Art Class Book Collection Promotes Better Reading," *Journal of Reading*, 1968, *11*,

333-336. How to gather and maintain a collection of books in an art classroom. The forerunner of the chapter on art in Thomas and Robinson's *Improving Reading in Every Class*.

Fleming, Natalie R. "Learning Centers in Elementary Art," *Art Teacher*, 1976, *6*, 10-12. The use of learning centers with specific suggestions for handling common problems. Illustrates one way to include purposeful reading in an art class.

Gainer, Ruth Straus. "The Arts Reader," *Art Education*, 1977, *30*, 33-38. Several activities designed to develop the ability to use mental imagery—an important aid to comprehension.

Henrichs, Margaret, Patty Baker, & Leandra Spangler. "Art Basics and Content Reading," *School Arts*, 1978, *78*, 26-29. Activities and techniques used by two junior high art teachers involved in a content area reading project.

Hoff, Gary R. "The Visual Narrative: Kids, Comic Books, and Creativity," *Art Education*, 1982, *35*, 20-23. Discussion of appeal of visual narratives to adolescents, and descriptions of how to use literature to motivate the creation of visual narratives.

Janoff, Barbara Haber. "Facilitating Interdisciplinary Learning," *Art Education*, 1976, *29*, 15-16. How to supplement crafts instruction with the reading of books and articles on the history of those crafts. Includes a bibliography and list of sources.

Manring, Barbara. "Discover Art History in the Classroom?" *Art Teacher*, 1974, *4*, 13-14. How to create "discovery boxes" containing letters, journal excerpts, and art works by artists being studied.

Mathias, Sandra L. Ess, & Mary E. Massa Fanyo. "Blending Reading Instruction with Music and Art," *Reading Teacher*, 1977, *30*, 497-500. Description of a program in which reading instruction was combined with art instruction.

O'Brien, Bernadette. "Art in the Reading Program," *Art Teacher*, 1976, *6*, 6-7. Description of two special programs in which reading instruction is combined with art instruction.

Peragallo, Anne M. "Incorporating Reading Skills into Art Lessons," *Art Education*, 1981, *34*, 31-35. Six activities designed to teach or reinforce reading skills through art activities.

Rabson, Barbara. "Reading and 'riting at the Guggenheim," *School Arts*, 1982, *81*, 13-15. Update on project described by O'Brien and Corwin. Address provided to write for more detailed information.

Richardson, Ann S. "Visual . . . Verbals, Here and Now," *Art Teacher*, 1976, *6*, 16-17. How to combine drawing and the language experience approach with children.

Sharknas, Jenevie. "Helping Kids Make Inferences," *Instructor*, 1976, *85*, 71-74. Description of an activity in which children make drawings that depict what the teacher is reading. Illustrates one approach to improving the ability to use mental imagery—an important aid to comprehension.

Business

Copeland, Amanda, & Lavelle Watkins. "Using Reference Materials," *Journal of Business Education*, 1979, *55*, 70-71. Discussion of the reference materials used by office workers and descriptions of several real-life activities for teaching use of those materials.

Frankhouser, Pamela L. "Proofreading: That Old Bugaboo!" *Balance Sheet*, 1979, *60*, 315-316. An approach for teaching proofreading in which students exchange papers to check each other's work.

Green, D. Hayden. "Realia: Tools for Consumer Education Instruction," *Balance Sheet*, 1974, *56*, 12-14, 36. Why and how to use objects, specimens, and samples, not just books, in teaching reading skills needed by consumers.

Harrison, Lincoln J. "Teaching Accounting Students to Read," *Journal of Business Education*, 1960, *35*, 169-170. Two techniques for helping students become more careful and more skilled in reading and solving accounting problems.

Humphreys, Nancy. "Filing—The Realistic Approach," *Balance Sheet*, 1981, *62*, 315-317, 331. Several activities for teaching filing—an important application of alphabetizing skills.

Johnson, Verda R. "Teaching for Better Understanding in Typewriting," *Journal of Business Education*, 1966, *41*, 149-150. Developing the ability to understand what is being typed and the ability to do library research on topics related to office work.

Lundgren, Carol A. "Make Proofreading Fun!" *Balance Sheet*, 1980, *62*, 42-44. A game type technique for teaching proofreading.

Misenoff, Ann. "STAR: Students' Typing and Reading," *Business Education Forum*, 1978, *33*, 5-7. A typing class for poor readers in which materials typed are on the reading and interest levels of the students.

Musselman, Vernon A. "The Reading Problem in Teaching Bookkeeping," *Business Education Forum*, 1959, *14*, 5-7. Several techniques for improving reading, emphasizing vocabulary building.

Peterson, John C., & John Staples. "Declare War on Undetected Typing Errors," *Business Education World*, 1969, *49*, 9-10, 22-24. Discussion of common types of errors, effective ways to proofread, and general guidelines for teaching proofreading.

Reiff, Rosanne. "Recognizing a Major Problem in Business Education—and Attempting to Solve It," *Balance Sheet*, 1975, *56*, 302-304. A variety of ways to attack reading problems and other language problems directly through business classes and through cooperation between English and business teachers.

Reiff, Rosanne. "Teaching the Art of Problem Solving," *Balance Sheet*, 1981, *62*, 225-227. Several activities for getting business students to think, including activities that improve or at least require thoughtful reading.

Schaefer, Julie C., & Edward Paradis. "Help the Student with Low Reading Ability," *Journal of Business Education*, 1977, *52*, 160-162. Several techniques for improving or motivating reading, including the use of Guide-O-Rama study guides, the use of special interest projects requiring reading, and efforts to provide supplementary materials at the reading levels of all students.

Schultheis, Robert A., & Kay Napoli. "Developing and Using Learning Activity Packages in Consumer Education: Part I," *Business Education Forum*, 1975, *29*, 16-19. How to prepare learning activity packages—an aid in meeting the needs of students with different reading abilities.

Schultheis, Robert A., & Kay Napoli. "Developing and Using Learning Activity Packages in Consumer Education: Part 2," *Business Education Forum*, 1975, *29*, 9-11. Continuation of the companion article.

Schultheis, Robert A., & Kay Napoli. "Strategies for Helping Poor Readers in Business Subjects," *Business Education Forum*,

1975, *30*, 5-12. A wide variety of approaches for dealing with reading problems.

Terrell, Marian N. "An Integrated Approach to English Skills," *Journal of Business Education*, 1981, *56*, 156-157. Techniques for building vocabulary and improving writing. Compiled from questionnaires completed by 45 business teachers.

Wingo, Rosetta. "Building Business Vocabulary through Intentional and Incidental Learning in Second Year Typing," *Business Education World*, 1977, *57*, 8-9, 29. A technique for building business vocabulary by having typing students type materials in which key business terms are defined.

Communication

Cox, Carole. "The Liveliest Art and Reading," *Language Arts*, 1976, *52*, 771-775, 807. The use of filmmaking projects to motivate and improve reading.

Deethardt, John F. "The Use of Questions in the Speech Communication Classroom," *Speech Teacher*, 1974, *23*, 15-20. Discussion of the appropriateness of speech communication classes for exposing students to higher-level questions.

Juleus, Nels G. "A Plan for Teaching Speech Preparation," *Speech Teacher*, 1965, *14*, 107-109. An approach that emphasizes the importance of planning before any search of written sources begins.

McCaleb, Joseph L. "Centering the Communication Course upon the Receiver of Persuasive Messages," *Communication Education*, 1977, *26*, 227-234. How to teach critical listening, which is related to critical reading.

McCroskey, James C. "Classroom Consequences of Communication Apprehension," *Communication Education*, 1977, *26*, 27-33. The causes and cures of communication fear, which can begin with a fear of oral reading.

Niles, Doris. "Recorder Projects for High School Speech Classes," *Speech Teacher*, 1967, *16*, 219-220. Ways to use a tape recorder in improving oral reading and other oral communication skills.

O'Shea, Catherine, & Margaret Egan. "A Primer of Drama Techniques for Teaching Literature," *English Journal*, 1978, *67*, 51-55. Suggestions for combining the reading of literature with a variety of dramatic techniques.

Post, Robert M. "Ensemble Oral Interpretation," *Speech Teacher*, 1974, *23*, 151-155. How to use group reading of literary selections.

Smale, Michael. "Teaching Secondary Students about Reading to Children," *Journal of Reading*, 1982, *26*, 208-210. Activities for teaching students why and how to read to children.

Solomon, Martha. "sips in the Speech Classroom," *Communication Education*, 1977, *26*, 270-273. How to construct and use self-instructional packets—a means of meeting individual needs and accommodating varying abilities.

Tucker, Betsy Rudelich. "Reading a Play," *Communications Education*, 1976, *25*, 103-110. How to teach the reading of plays.

Williams, Sheri S. "Building Listener Accountability," *Speech Teacher*, 1974, *23*, 53-56. Several activities for teaching listening skills.

English

Armelino, Barbara Ann. "Developing Critical Skills through Media Analysis," *English Journal*, 1979, *68*, 56-58. Teaching the analysis of advertising.

Backscheider, Paula. "Punctuation for the Reader: A Teaching Approach," *English Journal*, 1972, *61*, 874-877. How to teach punctuation by showing its importance to the reader.

Beach, Richard. "Conceiving of Characters," *Journal of Reading*, 1974, *17*, 546-551. Techniques for helping students learn to integrate information about characters in literary works.

Burroughs, Robert S. "Vocabulary Study and Context or How I Learned to Stop Worrying about Word Lists," *English Journal*, 1982, *71*, 53-55. An approach for building vocabulary emphasizing analysis of context.

Carlin, Jerome. "Your Next Book Report . . . , " *English Journal*, 1961, *50*, 16-22. Descriptions of a variety of book report formats.

Carroll, L. Patrick. "Those Pesky Book Reports," *Journal of Reading*, 1967, *10*, 468-472, 475. An approach to book reports that includes an objective test and options for topics to guide the writing of a brief essay.

Chesler, S. Alan. "Integrating the Teaching of Reading and Literature," *Journal of Reading*, 1976, *19*, 360-366. Activities for combining the teaching of a poem and the teaching of reading skills.

Clark, Wilma. "Twenty Hours of Activities in Vocabulary Building for High Potential Students," *English Journal*, 1981, *70*, 16-21. A variety of activities for building vocabulary.

Combs, Warren E. "Sentence-Combining Practice Aids Reading Comprehension," *Journal of Reading*, 1977, *21*, 18-24. Discussion of the effectiveness of sentence combining as a procedure for improving both writing and reading and descriptions of teaching activities.

Corley, Patricia. "Paperbacks: A Unit for Reading Appreciation," *Elementary English*, 1974, *51*, 421-423. A free-reading unit based on Daniel Fader's ideas about motivating reading.

Danielson, Earl R., Lesley A. Burrows, & David A. Rosenberg. "The Cassette Tape: An Aid to Individualizing High School English," *English Journal*, 1973, *62*, 441-445. The use of teacher made tape recordings of introductions and study guides for books to be read individually or in small groups.

Dilworth, Collett B. "The Reader as Poet: A Strategy for Creative Reading," *English Journal*, 1977, *66*, 43-47. Use of readiness activities in teaching poems.

Doemel, Nancy J. "Vocabulary for Slow Learners," *English Journal*, 1970, *59*, 78-80. A teaching approach in which the vocabulary instruction is blended into other instructional activities to provide the repetition and reinforcement needed by some students.

Donlan, Dan. "Developing a Reading Participation Guide for a Novel," *Journal of Reading*, 1974, *17*, 439-444. How to prepare a reading guide for a novel, using *Farenheit 451* as an example.

Donlan, Dan. "Developing a Participation Guide for a Play," *Journal of Reading*, 1975, *18*, 316-319. How to prepare a reading guide for a play, using *A Raisin in the Sun* as an example.

Donlan, Dan. "Multiple Text Programs in Literature," *Journal of Reading*, 1976, *19*, 312-319. How to prepare and use reading guides when students at different reading ability levels are studying different selections in a heterogeneous English class.

Dyer, Joyce. "Teaching the Disadvantaged: Teacher as Storyteller," *English Journal*, 1983, *72*, 72-74. How one teacher used storytelling to generate interest in reading.

Egan, Margaret, & Catherine O'Shea. "In Search of Motivation," *English Journal*, 1979, *68*, 33-35. How to use the multitext approach to literature instruction.

Evans, Ronald. "The Question about Literature," *English Journal*, 1982, *71*, 56-60. A list of generic questions for use with literary works and a discussion of reasons for using them.

Giermak, Elaine A. "Reading to High School Students: A Painless Method of Improving Language Skills," *English Journal*, 1980, *69*, 62-63. The use of *Black Boy* as the basis for listening activities designed to build language skills.

Haggard, Martha Rapp. "The Vocabulary Self-Collection Strategy: An Active Approach to Word Learning," *Journal of Reading*, 1982, *26*, 203-207. A strategy in which students individually suggest words and then as a group select the ones to study each week.

Howell, Suzanne. "Unlocking the Box: An Experiment in Literary Response," *English Journal*, 1977, *66*, 37-42. One teacher's first attempts at using a student response approach to literature instruction.

Howell, Suzanne. "The Research Paper *Redux*," *English Journal*, 1977, *66*, 52-55. Describes three research paper assignments designed to motivate and guide student reading and writing.

Hynes, Sister Nancy. "Learning to Read Short Stories," *Journal of Reading*, 1970, *13*, 429-432, 473. An approach involving teacher constructed study guides and student led small group discussion.

Kahle, David J. "Student-Centered Vocabulary," *English Journal*, 1972, *61*, 286-288. An approach for building vocabulary in which the students pick the words to be learned and then teach those words to their classmates.

Lent, John D. "Teaching the Cycle of Short Stories," *English Journal*, 1981, *70*, 55-57. How to teach literature by using anthologies of short stories by the same author. Illustrates a potentially effective approach for students who resist reading long novels.

Limbacher, James L. "Feature Films to Teach Literature," *English Journal*, 1981, *70*, 86-88. Use of films in teaching literature. Includes source information.

Lindquist, Alexa Ann. "Applying Bloom's Taxonomy in Writing Reading Guides for Literature," *Journal of Reading*, 1982,

25, 768-774. Discussion of the value of providing students with general reading guides for the major kinds of literature. Includes a general guide for reading a novel.

Marcus, Fred H. "A Modern Modest Proposal: Read the Movie First," *English Journal*, 1974, *63*, 94-97. How to use films to help students develop skills needed to understand and appreciate stories and longer works of literature.

Nieburger, Gayle D. "The Library and the English Program," *English Journal*, 1975, *64*, 83-84. Activities to help students become better, more frequent, and more appreciative library users.

O'Brien, Donald, & Sheila Schwarzberg. "A Strategy for Improving Teenagers' Understanding and Appreciation of Poetry," *Journal of Reading*, 1977, *20*, 381-386. The use of reading, reaction, and vocabulary extension guides in teaching poetry. Includes sample guides.

Odell, Lee. "Teaching Reading: An Alternative Approach," *English Journal*, 1973, *62*, 454-458, 488. Discusses need for helping students take the perspective of other people when reading literature, and describes teaching techniques for accomplishing that.

Peterson, Jean. "A Painless Approach to Vocabulary Building," *Instructor*, 1977, *87*, 86-88. Description of a weekly cycle of activities for building vocabulary in a heterogeneously grouped class.

Pietras, Thomas. "Teaching High School Literature: A Reading Skills Approach," *English Journal*, 1976, *65*, 44-47. How to use the directed reading activity with literature.

Poole, Val. "Outside Reading and Book Reporting," *English Journal*, 1981, *70*, 37. A technique for motivating outside reading that involves book reports written in class according to guidelines.

Post, Robert M. "Readers Theatre as a Method of Teaching Literature," *English Journal*, 1974, *63*, 69-72. Discussion of the use of readers theatre.

Probst, Robert E. "Response Based Teaching of Literature," *English Journal*, 1981, *70*, 43-47. Discussion of the response based approach to literature instruction.

Readence, John E., & Lyndon W. Searfoss. "Teaching Strategies for Vocabulary Development," *English Journal*, 1980, *69*, 43-

46. Three vocabulary building activities emphasizing categorization.

Sampson, Gloria Paulik, & Nancy Carlman. "A Hierarchy of Student Responses to Literature," *English Journal*, 1982, *71*, 54-57. An approach to leading discussions about short stories, based on the stages of student responses to literature.

Scheidler, Katherine P. "*Romeo and Juliet* and *The Glass Menagerie* as Reading Programs," *English Journal*, 1981, *70*, 34-36. How one teacher uses plays to teach a variety of reading skills.

Schiller, Charles. "I'm OK, You're OK: Let's Choral Read," *English Journal*, 1973, *62*, 791-794. Use of a form of reading that combines choral reading and readers theatre.

Sloane, Thomas O. "Readers Theatre Illusions and Classroom Realities," *English Journal*, 1977, *66*, 73-78. How to use readers theatre as an aid in teaching literature.

Small, Robert C., Jr. "The Junior Novel and the Art of Literature," *English Journal*, 1977, *66*, 56-59. The use of junior novels in teaching the reading of literature.

Stanford, Gene. "Word Study that Works," *English Journal*, 1971, *60*, 111-115. Evolution of one teacher's approach for teaching vocabulary that involves intensive study and extensive use of words being learned.

Stegall, Carrie. "Book Reports? Ugh!" *Language Arts*, 1975, *52*, 987-991. The use of short tests, rather than book reports, as a way for students to demonstrate that they have read a certain book.

Tashlik, Phyllis. "Introducing: Readers Theater," *Journal of Reading*, 1978, *22*, 216-219. How to use the oral reading of plays and adapted short stories.

Twining, James E. "Reading and Literature: The Heterogeneous Class," *Journal of Reading*, 1975, *18*, 475-480. Discussion of ways to accommodate varied student abilities and interests, including grouping and several types of activities to precede the reading of literary selections.

Webb, Agnes J. "Transactions with Literary Texts: Conversations in Classrooms," *English Journal*, 1982, *71*, 56-60. An approach to discussion of literary works that takes the form of conversations, not questioning.

White, Robert H. "Reading Skills in the English Class," *Clearing House*, 1977, *51*, 32-35. An approach for managing a combination of free reading, teacher directed, and independent skills work; individual and group project activities; and whole class instruction.

Williams, Lynnda. "Storytelling, Oral Literature or . . . Any Other Name Would Sound So Sweet," *English Journal*, 1982, *71*, 36-37. How to do an effective job of storytelling.

Zasadinski, Eugene. "Using Science Fiction to Build Research Skills," *English Journal*, 1983, *72*, 69-70. One teacher's use of science fiction to motivate interest in library research.

Foreign Languages

Birckbichler, Diane W., & Judith A. Muyskens. "A Personalized Approach to the Teaching of Literature at the Elementary and Intermediate Levels of Instruction," *Foreign Language Annals*, 1980, *13*, 23-27. A teaching approach in which students respond individually to literature.

Bornscheuer, Joan H. "Reading in a Foreign Language: A Many Splendored Thing," *Foreign Language Annals*, 1976, *9*, 304-306. The use of tapes and mimeograph sheets as guides accompanying reading selections.

Bourque, Jane, & Linda Chehy. "Exploratory Language and Culture," *Foreign Language Annals*, 1976, *9*, 10-16. Description of a junior high course in which some reading in English is done. Illustrates the potential role of foreign language classes in motivating voluntary reading.

Greenewald, M. Jane. "Setting Up an SSR Program in the Foreign Language Classroom: Some Questions and Answers," *Foreign Language Annals*, 1978, *11*, 293-296. How to use sustained silent reading.

Greenewald, M. Jane. "Developing and Using Cloze Materials to Teach Reading," *Foreign Language Annals*, 1981, *14*, 185-188. How to use the cloze procedure to help students develop sensitivity to semantic and syntactic information.

Hendon, Ursula S. "Introducing Culture in the High School Foreign Language Class," *Foreign Language Annals*, 1980, *13*, 191-199. A variety of activities for teaching the culture of the country whose language is being studied, including activities involving the reading of English. Illustrates potential role of foreign language classes in motivating voluntary reading.

Hosenfeld, Carol, et al. "Second Language Reading: A Curricular Sequence for Teaching Reading Strategies," *Foreign Language Annals*, 1981, *14*, 415-422. Activities for helping students identify and learn effective strategies for decoding foreign language texts.

Kramsch, Claire J. "Word Watching: Learning Vocabulary Becomes a Hobby," *Foreign Language Annals*, 1979, *12*, 153-158. A systematic, individualized teaching approach for vocabulary building.

Metz, Mary S. "An Audiolingual Methodology for Teaching Reading," *Foreign Language Annals*, 1973, *6*, 348-353. The use of a modified form of the directed reading activity in teaching reading selections.

Phillips, June K. "Second Language Reading: Teaching Decoding Skills," *Foreign Language Annals*, 1975, *8*, 227-232. Techniques for getting students to use context clues, structural clues, and other important clues in reading a second language.

Phillips, June K. "Reading is Communication, Too!" *Foreign Language Annals*, 1978, *11*, 281-287. How to teach foreign language reading as a real-life task of communication.

Schulz, Renate A. "From Word to Meaning: Foreign Language Reading Instruction after the Elementary Course," *Modern Language Journal*, 1983, *67*, 127-134. Discussion of teaching strategies for helping readers of foreign languages improve their psycholinguistic guessing skills.

Steiner, Florence. "Teaching Literature in the Secondary Schools," *Modern Language Journal*, 1972, *56*, 278-284. Discusses emphasizing ways to appeal to varied student interests and accommodate varied student abilities in teaching literature.

Strauber, Sandra K. "Language Learning Stations," *Foreign Language Annals*, 1981, *14*, 31-36. How to use learning centers—one way to accommodate varied needs and abilities.

Health
Allegrante, John P. "Well-Read and Healthy," *Health Education*, 1975, *6*, 35-36. Discusses ways the *New York Times* can serve as a resource for students and teachers.

Beyrer, Mary K. "Popular Literature: A Rich Resource for Health Education," *Journal of Health, Physical Education, and Recreation*, 1961, *32*, 31-32. Discussion of use of popular literature and a bibliography of books.

Dunning, H. Neal. "Nutrition Labeling: A New Educational Tool," *School Health Review*, 1974, *5*, 12-15. Discussion of nutrition labels and how to teach them.

Glaros, Timothy. "Breaking the Language Barrier," *Health Education*, 1977, *8*, 39-40. Use of prefixes, suffixes, and roots in teaching vocabulary.

Grubaugh, Steven, & Roy Molesworth, Jr. "Teaching Vocabulary and Developing Concepts in Health," *Journal of Reading*, 1980, *23*, 420-423. Description of a values oriented strategy for teaching vocabulary and concepts.

Hals, Elaine. "Stress on Reading," *Health Education*, 1979, *10*, 33. Discussion of varied teaching techniques that can improve reading.

Kime, Robert E., & William T. Jarvis. "Consumer Health: A Difficult Teaching Area?" *School Health Review*, 1973, *4*, 6-9. Discussion of the teaching of consumer health, emphasizing techniques for teaching the reading of advertisements.

Pruitt, B. E. "The Open Contract: A Program of Individualized Study," *Health Education*, 1975, *6*, 37-38. An approach in which individual students select topics and investigate them individually or in small groups.

Scheer, Judith K., & Glay Williams. "Using Children's Stories to Teach 'Something We Don't Talk About' (Death Education)," *Health Values*, 1977, *1*, 120-126. An approach for teaching death education using children's literature.

Home Economics

Bengston, Anne, & Linda Flick. "Teaching the Three Rs through Home Economics," *Forecast for Home Economics*, 1978, *23*, 37, 60. Descriptions of several teaching strategies that can improve reading.

Cibrowski, Lee. "Coping with Student Illiteracy," *Forecast for Home Economics*, 1980, *26*, 29, 60. Descriptions of several teaching strategies that can improve reading.

Cochran, Nancy K. "Nutrition and World Literature," *Forecast for Home Economics*, 1981, *26*, 59. Describes an interdisciplinary course on eating customs as reflected in world literature.

Dieffenderfer, Ruth I. "Teaching Reading Through Crafts," *Forecast for Home Economics*, 1974, *19*, 14-15. Description of an elective course in which students learn to read directions in order to carry out sewing projects.

Frick, Lucille. "An Effective Self-Instructional Strategy for Secondary Students," *Illinois Teacher of Home Economics*, 1981, *24*, 189-190. How to prepare learning centers—a way to accommodate varied needs and abilities.

Jefferson, Elizabeth, & Daisy Rice. "Improving Teens' Self-Image through Reading," *School Library Journal*, 1975, *21*, 78. Describes a program in which students learn to read to children and practice their skills as part of a child development unit.

Ludden, Mary C. "Elementary Home Economics and Children's Literature," *Journal of Home Economics*, 1976, *68*, 17-21. An approach in which children's literature is used in teaching home economics topics.

Shear, Twyla, & Elizabeth Ray. "Home Economics Learning Packages," *Journal of Home Economics*, 1969, *61*, 768-770. How to prepare and use learning packages—a way to accommodate varying needs and abilities.

Smale, Michael. "Teaching Secondary Students about Reading to Children," *Journal of Reading*, 1982, *26*, 208-210. A series of activities for teaching students why and how to read to children.

Stewart, Marjorie S. "Another Look at Independent Study," *What's New in Home Economics*, 1971, *35*, 20. Discussion of the use of library research projects.

Wagener, Elaine H. "Recipe for Reading Comprehension," *Journal of Reading*, 1977, *20*, 498-502. How recipes can be used in improving reading.

Industrial Arts

Allen, Irene Amilhat, & Kendall N. Starkweather. "Develop Reading Skills by Focusing on Change," *Man/Society/Technology*, 1971, *31*, 92-95. Discussion of the use of library research projects.

Baillargeon, Jarvis. "Graphic Arts Spawns a RATPAC of Readers," *School Shop*, 1979, *38*, 28-29. Update of project described by Siegel.

Conroy, Michael T. "Project Bookmark: Reading and Graphic Arts," *Journal of Reading*, 1971, *15*, 60-61. A set of activities for making reading an important part of a graphic arts class.

Conroy, Michael T. "Teaching Reading Skills in Industrial Arts," *Industrial Education*, 1979, *68*, 22-23. The use of charts for teaching vocabulary.

Conroy, Michael T. "Instructional Sheets for Students with Reading Difficulties," *Industrial Education*, 1979, *68*, 32-34. How to prepare readable instruction sheets.

Conroy, Michael T. "Reading and Following Printed Directions," *Industrial Education*, 1980, *69*, 24-28. A lesson on following written directions.

Conroy, Michael T. "Reference Book for Your Shop Library," *Industrial Education*, 1981, *70*, 14-15. An activity in which students prepare research reports on topics selected by them. The reports in a specific area are bound together as a reference book.

Ferrerio, Anthony. "Try Industrial Arts and Vocational Education for Retarded Readers," *Industrial Arts and Vocational Education*, 1960, *49*, 19-20. Descriptions of a variety of techniques for teaching vocabulary.

Hall, Lucien T., Jr. "Reading Graduated Scales," *Mathematics Teacher*, 1982, *75*, 34-36. How to teach the reading of thermometers, speedometers, rulers, and other graduated scales.

Hird, Kenneth F. "Learning Activity Packages for Competency Based Instruction," *School Shop*, 1979, *38*, 28-29. How to prepare learning activity packages.

Mikulecky, Larry, & William Diehl. "Help Your Kids with Their Reading," *Industrial Education*, 1979, *68*, 28, 30. Descriptions of several strategies for improving reading.

Millman, Gerald. "Build Vocabulary in the Shop," *School Shop*, 1980, *40*, 17. Description of a vocabulary building technique based on word roots.

Pearson, Herbert, & Ellen Lamar Thomas. "If Your Classes Have Trouble Reading Instructions . . . ," *Industrial Education*, 1974, *63*, 22-23. An approach in which students are taught a set of guidelines on following directions.

Ryan, Ray D., & Wayne Berry. "Motivate Your Students with Independent Studies," *Industrial Education*, 1975, *64*, 26-27. An approach in which individual students occasionally select a topic of special interest, investigate that topic, and often complete a hands-on project related to the topic.

Siegel, Herb, & staff. "Johnny Can Read—and Publish Too!" *Industrial Education*, 1974, *63*, 38-39. Describes a project in which elementary industrial arts students publish their own writing.

Walenick, Vincent J., Joseph Kobylarz, & George J. Baskinger. "Reading and IA Skills Make Not-So-Strange Bedfellows," *School Shop*, 1978, *38*, 20-21, 23. Descriptions of activities combining reading and drafting.

Library Services

Biggs, Mary. "A Proposal for Course Related Library Instruction," *School Library Journal*, 1980, *26*, 34-37. How to help students learn library research skills during library projects.

Chelton, Mary K. "Booktalking: You Can Do It," *School Library Journal*, 1976, *22*, 39-43. How to do booktalks to interest students in specific books.

Davis, Dorothy Voight. "Book Clubs in the Middle Grades," *Journal of Reading*, 1975, *19*, 150-153. Discussion of the use of parent led book clubs.

DeLooza, Diane E. "Students' Comment Boxes," *School Library Journal*, 1981, *27*, 34. A procedure for letting students know what other students think about books.

Elza, Betty, & Diana Owatt. "Turning to Individualized Instruction: Reading in the Round," *Journal of Reading*, 1975, *19*, 125-127. A structured individualized reading program for advanced readers, based in the school library.

Fusco, Esther. "Portable Paperbacks," *School Library Journal*, 1982, *28*, 44. Description of a portable bookstore run by students in basic English classes and stocked with books selected by students.

Hadden, Margaret S. "Mid-Year Blahs? Try a Reading Contest," *School Library Journal*, 1979, *25*, 42. Describes the use of a contest to motivate reading.

Herber, Harold L. "Librarians in the All-School Reading Program," *Wilson Library Bulletin*, 1976, *50*, 715-718. Discusses role of librarian in a content area reading program.

Janney, Kay Print. "Introducing Oral Interpretation in Elementary School," *Reading Teacher*, 1980, *33*, 544-547. Description of a program in which students read to younger children in the library.

Kline, Carol. "Planning Problem-Free Book Fairs," *School Library Journal*, 1977, *23*, 36-40. How to plan and run a book fair to sell books.

Kuenzer, Kathy. "Junior Great Books: An Interpretive Reading Program," *School Library Journal*, 1978, *24*, 32-34. How to organize an interpretive reading program in a library.

Mahoney, Sally. "Individualizing in the Library," *Elementary English*, 1975, *52*, 346-350, 375. How to prepare reading projects to be completed individually by able students in the library.

Miller, Margaret J. "Can't Keep Them Out of the Library," *Early Years*, 1977, *7*, 30-31, 60. Several techniques for getting young children to use a school library.

Portteus, Elnora M. "Cleveland's Media Centers Go All Out for Reading," *Wilson Library Bulletin*, 1976, *50*, 725-727. Describes several ways in which school libraries in Cleveland cooperate in the reading program.

Reed, Barbara. "A Reading Promotion Event for YAS," *School Library Journal*, 1982, *28*, 111-112. Describes high school activities that are part of a reading promotion week in one school district.

Rowe, Sula J. "Independent Reading," *English Journal*, 1983, *72*, 35-36. Describes an independent reading program organized by a librarian for students in a K-12 school.

Ryder, Sarah. "Living Under Water with Disadvantaged Juniors," *Journal of Reading*, 1968, *11*, 268-270, 306. The use of book talks with English classes.

Scales, Pat. "Spotlighting Readers and Writers," *School Library Journal*, 1976, *23*, 75-79. Describes an activity in which students have conference phone calls with authors.

Singer, Dorothy G. "Television 'Tie-Ins' in the School Library," *School Library Journal*, 1979, *26*, 51-52. Ways to take advantage of television as a reading motivator.

Wilmer, Kathryn G. "Mystery at the Library," *School Library Journal*, 1982, *28*, 24-26. An activity for teaching library research skills that involves solving a mystery.

Witt, Lois M. "Practical Tips for Operating a Paperback Store," *School Library Journal*, 1981, *27*, 37. How to operate a paperback store.

Witucke, Virginia. "The Book Talk: A Technique for Bringing Together Children and Books," *Language Arts*, 1979, *56*, 413-421. How to use a book talk to generate interest in a book.

Mathematics

Crouse, Richard. "Ripley's Believe It or Not—A Source of Motivational Incentives," *Mathematics Teacher*, 1974, *67*, 107-109.

The use of interesting facts to introduce units and motivate reading of the textbook.

Crouse, Richard, & Denise Bassett. "Detective Stories: An Aid for Mathematics and Reading," *Mathematics Teacher*, 1975, *68*, 598-600. The use of minute mysteries to teach deductive reasoning.

Davidson, James. "The Language Experience Approach to Story Problems," *Arithmetic Teacher*, 1977, *25*, 28. Description of an approach in which students write their own story problems.

Denmark, Tom. "Improving Students' Comprehension of Word Problems," *Mathematics Teacher*, 1983, *76*, 31-34. Four exercises for improving reading of word problems.

Dittrich, Alan B. "An Experiment in Teaching the History of Mathematics," *Mathematics Teacher*, 1973, *66*, 35-38. A semester course illustrating the potential of history to motivate interest in mathematics. Suggests one way to include the reading of prose in a mathematics class.

Esbenshade, Donald H., Jr. "Adding Dimension to *Flatland*: A Novel Approach to Geometry," *Mathematics Teacher*, 1983, *76*, 120-123. How one teacher uses the science fiction book *Flatland* in a geometry class.

Feeman, George F. "Reading and Mathematics," *Arithmetic Teacher*, 1973, *20*, 523-529. Strategies for improving the reading of mathematics, including the use of study guides.

Fennell, Francis. "The Newspaper: A Source for Applications in Mathematics," *Arithmetic Teacher*, 1982, *30*, 22-26. Activities for combining the reading of newspapers and the reinforcement of math skills.

Garf, David. "Some Techniques in Handling a Slow Class in Elementary Algebra," *Mathematics Teacher*, 1972, *65*, 591-594. Describes a program in a class for which the book was too difficult, involving students copying a "primer" from the board.

Hall, Lucien T., Jr. "Reading Graduated Scales," *Mathematics Teacher*, 1982, *75*, 34-36. How to teach the reading of thermometers, speedometers, rulers, and other graduated scales.

Henny, Maribeth. "Improving Mathematics Verbal Problem Solving Ability through Reading Instruction," *Arithmetic Teach-

er, 1971, *18*, 223-229. An approach for improving the ability to solve word problems.

Henrichs, Margaret, & Tom Sisson. "Mathematics and the Reading Process: A Practical Application of Theory," *Mathematics Teacher*, 1980, *73*, 253-257. Describes coordinated efforts to improve reading through mathematics in a Missouri junior high school.

Krist, Betty J., Mary Ellen O'Neil, & Lawrence Feldman. "Support Your Local Library: A Task Card Project for Mathematics Students," *Mathematics Teacher*, 1980, *73*, 516-518. An approach in which students search for answers to mathematics questions by referring to books on library reserve.

Krulik, Stephen. "Learning Packages for Mathematics Instruction—Some Considerations," *Mathematics Teacher*, 1974, *67*, 348-351. The preparation and use of learning activity packages—a way to accommodate varying needs and abilities.

Krulik, Stephen. "To Read or Not To Read, That Is the Question!" *Mathematics Teacher*, 1980, *73*, 248-252. Techniques for improving the reading of mathematics.

Lacey, Patrick A., & Philip E. Weil. "Number—Reading—Language!" *Language Arts*, 1975, *52*, 776-782. Suggestions for teaching the reading of math symbols.

LeBlanc, John F. "Teaching Textbook Story Problems," *Arithmetic Teacher*, 1982, *29*, 52-54. How to teach an approach to the solving of word problems.

Maffei, Anthony. "Reading Analysis in Mathematics," *Journal of Reading*, 1973, *16*, 546-549. Describes a variation of the PQ4R study method for solving word problems.

Montague, Harriet F. "Let Your Students Write a Book," *Mathematics Teacher*, 1973, *66*, 548-550. A special program in which able students wrote a book on matrix algebra.

Munro, John. "Language Abilities and Maths Performance," *Reading Teacher*, 1979, *32*, 900-915. Some of the basic problems that children have in reading mathematical materials, and techniques for dealing with those problems.

Nibbelink, William. "Graphing for Any Grade," *Arithmetic Teacher*, 1982, *30*, 28-31. A step-by-step approach for teaching the construction and reading of graphs.

Osborne, Ursula. "Individualized Mathematics: A Simple Approach," *Mathematics Teacher*, 1976, *69*, 390-395. A program for accommodating the varying needs and abilities of remedial students.

Pachtman, Andrew B., & James D. Riley. "Teaching the Vocabulary of Mathematics through Interaction, Exposure, and Structure," *Journal of Reading*, 1978, *22*, 240-244. The use of structured overviews in teaching the vocabulary used in word problems. Includes a sample.

Radebaugh, Muriel Rogie. "Using Children's Literature to Teach Mathematics," *Reading Teacher*, 1981, *34*, 902-906. The use of children's literature in teaching basic mathematical concepts. Includes a resource list.

Riley, James D., & Andrew B. Pachtman. "Reading Mathematical Word Problems: Telling Them What to Do Is Not Telling Them How to Do It," *Journal of Reading*, 1978, *21*, 531-534. The use of reading guides in teaching word problems. Includes a sample guide.

Slaughter, Judith Pollard. "The Graph Examined," *Arithmetic Teacher*, 1983, *30*, 41-45. How to teach the reading of graphs.

Woerner, Kathy. "The High School Mathematics Research Paper," *Mathematics Teacher*, 1977, *70*, 448-451. The use of a research paper as a requirement in advanced classes.

Woolfe, Maryanne T. "The Math/Reading Skills Connection," *Teacher*, 1980, *97*, 76-78. Use of children's literature to generate interest in math.

Music

Bowren, Fay F. "Words, Structure, and Visual Perception: An Obstacle Course in Music Learning," *Music Educators Journal*, 1972, *58*, 54-57. Discussion of some of the reading demands facing students in music, and ways for teachers to deal with those demands.

Debban, Betty. "The Direct Link in Reading Readiness," *Music Educators Journal*, 1977, *63*, 42-45. How to teach a listening understanding of music concepts; notation is introduced gradually.

Earle, Richard, & Linda Perney. "Reading the Words in Music Class," *Music Educators Journal*, 1972, *59*, 55-56. How to prepare students for reading the lyrics of songs.

Hainen, Judith. "Make Room for Learning Centers," *Music Educators Journal*, 1977, *63*, 46-49. The use of learning centers. Illustrates one way to include purposeful reading in a music class.

Hickman, David R. "Music Speed Reading," *Instrumentalist*, 1980, *34*, 32-33. Description of an approach for improving sight reading using speed reading techniques.

Hicks, Charles E. "Sound before Sight: Strategies for Teaching Music Reading," *Music Educators Journal*, 1980, *66*, 53-55, 65, 67. Expansion of ideas in O'Brien.

Lloyd, Mavis J. "Teach Music to Aid Beginning Readers," *Reading Teacher*, 1978, *32*, 323-327. Instructional activities in music that can contribute to reading improvement.

Mathias, Sandra L. Ess, & Mary E. Massa Fanyo. "Blending Reading Instruction with Music and Art," *Reading Teacher*, 1977, *30*, 497-500. Description of a program in which reading instruction was combined with music instruction.

O'Brien, James P. "Teach the Principles of Notation, Not Just the Symbols," *Music Educators Journal*, 1974, *60*, 38-42. How to teach the principles of music notation before the symbols. Corresponds to the instructional practice in reading of teaching well the meaning of a word before working intensively on visual recognition of the word.

Peotter, Jean. "Contracts," *Music Educators Journal*, 1975, *61*, 46-49. Discussion of the use of an individual projects approach in which reading plays a major role.

Phelan, Elizabeth S. "Teaching Language Skills in the General Music Class," *Music Educators Journal*, 1965, *51*, 176-178. Techniques for improving reading and other language skills.

Reeves, Harriet R. "Building Basic Skills with Music," *Music Educators Journal*, 1978, *65*, 74-79. Activities for improving reading and reading readiness skills through music.

Rodean, Richard W. "Comparative Music Survey: An Integration of the Arts," *Music Educators Journal*, 1965, *51*, 55-56. Describes a high school music course in history, theory, and related topics studied through library sources. Illustrates the potential benefits of using supplementary reading in music classes.

Sotos, George, & Kathi Macdonald. "Of Magazines and Music," *Instrumentalist*, 1978, *33*, 76. The use of a magazine rack in a bandroom to motivate reading.

Willard, Raymond. "Sight Reading for Young Students," *Instrumentalist*, 1980, *34*, 24-25. An approach based on the principle of gradually increasing the complexity of materials to be sight read—a principle that has its counterpart in reading instruction.

Physical Education

Aufsesser, Kathryn Summa. "Beyond the Ordinary: Learning Centers in Elementary Physical Education," *Journal of Physical Education and Recreation*, 1980, *51*, 36-38. How to use learning centers—a good way to incorporate reading into physical education instruction.

Baust, Joseph A., Sr. "Teaching Spatial Relationships Using Language Arts and Physical Education," *School Science and Mathematics*, 1982, *82*, 603-606. Techniques for teaching spatial concepts using physical activities.

Gilbert, Anne Green. "Dance: A Nonverbal Approach to Learning the Three R's," *Journal of Physical Education and Recreation*, 1979, *50*, 58-60. Activities related to rhyming, punctuation, and phonics.

James, Helen J. "Building Reading Vocabulary in PE and Health Classes," *Journal of Physical Education and Recreation*, 1977, *48*, 56-57. Activity oriented techniques for teaching vocabulary.

Kravitz, Richard, & Marvin Shapiro. "Reading-Boxing Class," *Journal of Health, Physical Education, and Recreation*, 1969, *40*, 26-29. A special class that illustrates ways to combine physical education and reading.

Maring, Gerald H., & Robert Ritson. "Reading Improvement in the Gymnasium," *Journal of Reading*, 1980, *24*, 27-31. Strategies for improving reading through physical education.

Thomas, Ellen L. "Books Are the Greatest," *Journal of Reading*, 1968, *12*, 119-124. Description of one teacher's strategies for motivating reading. The forerunner of the chapter on physical education in Thomas and Robinson's *Improving Reading in Every Class*.

Science

Black, Jon Timothy, & Iola W. Harding. "Developing Reading Skills in the High School Physics Class," *Physics Teacher*, 1981, *19*, 106-112. Strategies for improving reading, including the use of a minilibrary of multilevel textbooks.

Castallo, Richard, & Douglas Llewellyn. "Learning to Follow Directions," *Science and Children*, 1975, *13*, 32-34. A set of procedures for identifying deficiencies and for teaching students how to follow directions.

Cimino, John, & Pascal de Caprariis. "Updating and Personalizing a High School Earth Science Program," *Journal of Geological Education*, 1976, *24*, 21-22. A program involving multiple sources and the rewriting of materials.

Cochran, Cheryl. "Science–Reading Kits," *Science and Children*, 1979, *17*, 12-13. An approach in which students create learning packets.

Collins, B. Kevin. "Independent Projects: An Organized Approach," *American Biology Teacher*, 1981, *43*, 463-465. How to organize the use of independent projects in biology, including library research projects.

Cornett, Charles. "Reading for Fun . . . in Science Class?" *Science Teacher*, 1975, *42*, 58-59. Describes a program of weekly free reading.

Daugs, Donald R. "What Price Success, Multilevel Science," *Science Education*, 1971, *55*, 569-572. Discussion of the use of multilevel texts in science.

Deck, Ray F. "Vocabulary Development to Improve Reading and Achievement in Science," *American Biology Teacher*, 1952, *14*, 13-15. An approach for teaching the key words in a science unit.

DeLorenzo, Ronald. "Simple Techniques to Generate Chemical Applications that Arouse Student Interest," *Journal of Chemical Education*, 1982, *59*, 531-532. The use of science magazines in locating information to use as teaching illustrations and as content for problems.

Esler, William K., & King Merritt, Jr. "Teaching Reading through Science Experience Stories," *School Science and Mathematics*, 1976, *76*, 203-206. An approach in which science activities lead to language experience stories.

Gavenas, Emil. "Scavenger Hunt: A Teaching Tool to Reinforce the Basics," *American Biology Teacher*, 1981, *43*, 272-273. A strategy for reinforcing learning of key biological concepts.

Guerra, Cathy L., & DeLores B. Payne. "Using Popular Books and Magazines to Interest Students in General Science," *Journal of Reading*, 1981, *24*, 583-586. How to use popular books and magazines to motivate students.

Hall, Lucien T., Jr. "Reading Graduated Scales," *Mathematics Teacher*, 1982, *75*, 34-36. How to teach the reading of thermometers, speedometers, rulers, and other graduated scales.

Janke, Delmar, & Donna Norton. "Science Trades in the Classroom: Good Tools for Teachers," *Science and Children*, 1983, *20*, 46-48. How to select science trade books and use them in the classroom. Includes brief descriptions of several activities.

Kosmoski, Sister Leandra. "Children's Literature in the Science Class," *Science and Children*, 1980, *18*, 10-11. An approach in which students read tradebooks related to science and then write their own science books.

Krockover, Gerald H. "Developing Earth Science Modules for the Secondary School," *Journal of Geological Education*, 1977, *25*, 115-117. Discussion of the use of modules.

Mettes, C.T.C.W., A. Pilot, H.J. Roossink, & H. Kramers-Pals. "Teaching and Learning Problem Solving in Science," *Journal of Chemical Education*, 1980, *57*, 882-885. Description of an approach for teaching students how to solve problems.

Milligan, Jerry L., & Donald C. Orlich. "A Linguistic Approach to Learning Science Vocabulary," *Science Teacher*, 1981, *48*, 34-35. Discussion of the use of prefixes, roots, and suffixes in teaching vocabulary.

Norton, Donna, & Delmar Janke. "Improving Science Reading Ability," *Science and Children*, 1983, *20*, 5-8. Activities for using trade books to improve science reading skills.

Oakley, Donald L. "Your Feet and Friction: A Reading-Science Unit," *Science and Children*, 1972, *10*, 22-24. An activity for teaching reading for details and following directions.

Orlich, Donald C., Richard F. Gebhardt, Rosalie Harms, & Georgina Lee Ward. "Science Learning Centers: An Aid to Instruction," *Science and Children*, 1982, *20*, 18-20. How to construct and use learning centers. Includes brief descriptions of several sample centers.

Rydzewski, Sister Mary Marcia. "Using the Multitext Approach in the Junior High School," *Science Teacher*, 1974, *41*, 39-40. An approach in which a variety of books on each subject are used, rather than multiple copies of one text.

Telfer, Richard, & Don Moore. "Improving Reading in Individualized Science," *Science Teacher*, 1975, *42*, 22. An approach involving the use of rewritten versions of key textbook passages, simplified explanations that supplement the textbook, and other teacher-constructed materials.

Tocci, Salvatore. "A Flexible, Individualized Approach to Instruction Using the BSCS *Yellow* Version," *American Biology Teacher*, 1981, *43*, 148-151. An approach involving learning activity packages—one way to accommodate varying needs and abilities.

van Deuren, Arnold E. "Improving Basic Skills in the Modified Science Classroom," *American Biology Teacher*, 1979, *41*, 471-474. Strategies suitable for use with poor readers.

Warren, Robert. "Helping Poor Readers in Secondary Science," *Science Teacher*, 1975, *42*, 55. How to prepare and use tapes of textbook chapters.

Wright, Jill D., & Paul B. Hounshell. "Enhance Reading through Science," *Science Teacher*, 1978, *45*, 34-36. Teaching strategies for improving reading.

Wright, John L. "The Novel as a Device for Motivating Junior High Science Students," *American Biology Teacher*, 1979, *41*, 502-504. Discussion of how *Julie of the Wolves* might be used.

Social Studies

Allen, Rodney F., & David E. LaHart. "Critical Thinking Skills and Energy: Using Energy Error Cards in Geography Classes," *Journal of Geography*, 1981, *80*, 64-70. An activity for teaching critical thinking. Includes sample materials.

Cline, Ruth K. J., & Bob L. Taylor. "Integrating Literature and 'Free Reading' into the Social Studies Program," *Social Education*, 1978, *42*, 27-31. Discussion of the use of supplementary books.

Cohan, Mark. "Comic Books in the Classroom," *Social Education*, 1975, *39*, 324-325. Ways to use comic books in teaching important social studies topics.

Devan, Steven, Rozalyn Klein, & Terrence V. Murphy. "Priming—A Method to Equalize Differences between High and Low Achievement Students," *Journal of Reading*, 1975, *19*, 143-146. A procedure to equalize the reading demands on poor and good readers in an inquiry based assignment.

Downey, Matthew T. "Childhood: The Way It Was," *Teacher*, 1980, *98*, 59, 61-62. Using memoirs of pioneer children taken from autobiographies of early settlers. Illustrates one way to make reading in history more interesting to students.

Duscher, Raymond. "How to Help Social Science Students Read Better," *Social Studies*, 1975, *66*, 258-261. Strategies for improving reading, including grouping by reading level.

Ferguson, Jack. "Using Road Maps in the Junior High School," *Journal of Geography*, 1976, *75*, 570-574. A series of activities for teaching map reading.

Fernald, Edward, Jesse Lott, & John Lunstrum. "Relating Background to Comprehension through Word Association and Value Examination: A Case Study in Geography," *Social Education*, 1978, *42*, 21-23. An activity to motivate and prepare students to read an assignment.

Frankel, Jill Catherine. "Reading Skills through Social Studies Content and Student Involvement," *Journal of Reading*, 1974, *18*, 23-26. Description of a seventh grade class in which language experience, games, drama, and other nontraditional techniques were used.

Glenn, Allen D., & Edith West. "Using the Textbook and Reading Materials More Effectively in the Social Studies Classroom," *Social Studies*, 1980, *71*, 163-167. Five options for accommodating students at varied reading levels in the same class.

Haas, Mary E. "Around the Map: A Game for Practicing Map Skills," *Journal of Geography*, 1980, *79*, 196-197. Description of a game for practicing map reading skills.

Hash, Ronald J., & Mollie B. Bailey. "A Classroom Strategy: Improving Social Studies Comprehension," *Social Education*, 1978, *42*, 24-26. How to prepare a three level reading guide.

Klasky, Charles. "The History Mystery," *Social Studies*, 1979, *70*, 41-43. An activity combining library research, writing, and careful reading for details.

Kratzner, Roland R., & Nancy Mannies. "Building Responsibility and Reading Skills in the Social Studies Classroom," *Journal of Reading*, 1979, *22*, 501-505. An approach in which students individually select topics to investigate and tasks to perform when investigating the topics and reporting their findings.

Larkin, James M., & Jane J. White. "The Learning Center in the Social Studies Classroom," *Social Education*, 1974, *38*, 698-710. How to plan and use learning centers. Includes detailed descriptions of two sample centers.

Lott, Jesse. "Classroom Journals," *Social Education*, 1978, *42*, 15-17. Description of the use of student journals as an aid in motivating reading and building vocabulary.

Lunstrum, John P., & Judith L. Irvin. "Integration of Basic Skills into Social Studies Content," *Social Education*, 1981, *45*, 169-177. Using the directed reading activity. Includes a sample lesson built around primary source materials.

Lunstrum, John P. "Building Motivation through the Use of Controversy," *Journal of Reading*, 1981, *24*, 687-691. An activity that uses controversy to generate motivation for reading and discussion.

McGoldrick, James H. "Using Novels in History Class," *Social Studies*, 1963, *54*, 95-97. Discussion of the use of novels. Includes a sample study guide.

Mikulecky, Larry, & Frederick Smith. "Independence and Elaboration Day: Activities to Enhance Student Reading in Social Studies," *Social Studies*, 1981, *72*, 69-71. Activities used on special days to get students interested in reading beyond the textbook and to acquaint them with "real world" printed materials related to social studies topics.

O'Connor, John R. "Reading Skills in the Social Studies," *Social Education*, 1967, *31*, 104-107. Discussion of several teaching techniques to help poor readers.

Rader, William D. "Improving Critical Reading through Consumer Education," *Social Education*, 1978, *42*, 18-20. How to improve the critical reading of advertisements.

Sandberg, Kate. "Learning to Read History Actively," *Journal of Reading*, 1981, *25*, 158-160. An approach to reading history that is a modification of the scientific method of problem solving.

Schneider, Donald O., & Mary Jo M. Brown. "Helping Students Study and Comprehend Their Social Studies Textbooks," *Social Education*, 1980, *44*, 105-112. Strategies to use before, during, and after the reading of chapters. Includes sample reading guides.

Solovy, David A. "The Teaching of Reading in Social Studies," *Social Studies*, 1975, *66*, 80-82. Techniques for improving and motivating reading.

Stein, Harry. "The Visual Reading Guide," *Social Education*, 1978, *42*, 534-535. A procedure in which students work individually and then as a class to preview reading assignments by examining graphic aids in the assignment.

Stine, Doris E. "Tenth Grade Content—Fourth Grade Reading Level," *Journal of Reading*, 1971, *14*, 559-561. The procedures used in a world cultures class containing mainly poor readers.

Thomas, Ellen Lamar, & Philip Montag. "A Social Studies Department Talks Back," *Journal of Reading*, 1966, *10*, 22-28. Ways to match materials to the reading abilities of individual students. Some of the same ideas are found in the chapter on social studies in Thomas and Robinson's *Improving Reading in Every Class*.

Tiedt, Sidney W., & Iris M. Tiedt. "Teaching Current Events," *Social Studies*, 1967, *58*, 112-114. Strategies for making the study of current events more interesting. Illustrates one way to use newspapers and magazines as supplementary materials.

Turner, Thomas N. "Making the Social Studies Textbook a More Effective Tool for Less Able Readers," *Social Education*, 1976, *40*, 38-41. Techniques for helping students learn from their textbooks.

Yeager, Tina A., & Catherine W. Edwards. "The Textbook: A Source for Activities," *Social Education*, 1980, *44*, 113-114. Activities for varying the way textbook chapters are used.

Books—Bibliography

Aukerman, Robert C. *Reading in the Secondary School Classroom*. New York: McGraw-Hill, 1972.

Bechtel, Judith, & Bettie Franzblau. *Reading in the Science Classroom*. Washington, D.C.: National Education Association, 1980.

Bristow, Page S., & Alan E. Farstrup. *Reading in Health/Physical Education/Recreation Classes*. Washington, D.C.: National Education Association, 1981.

Bullock, Terry L., & Karl Hesse. *Reading in the Social Studies Classroom*. Washington, D.C.: National Education Association, 1981.

Cowen, John E. (Ed.). *Teaching Reading through the Arts*. Newark, Delaware: International Reading Association, 1983.

Cunningham, James W., Patricia M. Cunningham, & Sharon V. Arthur. *Middle and Secondary School Reading*. New York: Longman, 1981.

Duffy, Gerald G. (Ed.). *Reading in the Middle School*. Newark, Delaware: International Reading Association, 1974.

Earle, Richard A. *Teaching Reading and Mathematics*. Newark, Delaware: International Reading Association, 1976.

Gentile, Lance. *Using Sports and Physical Education to Strengthen Reading Skills*. Newark, Delaware: International Reading Association, 1980.

Graves, Michael F., Rebecca J. Palmer, & David W. Furniss. *Structuring Reading Activities for English Classes*. Urbana, Illinois: National Council of Teachers of English, 1976.

Hafner, Lawrence E. *Developmental Reading in Middle and Secondary Schools*. New York: Macmillan, 1977.

Laffey, James L. (Ed.). *Reading in the Content Areas*. Newark, Delaware: International Reading Association, 1972.

Lamberg, Walter J., & Charles E. Lamb. *Reading Instruction in the Content Areas*. Chicago: Rand McNally, 1980.

Lundstrum, John P., & Bob Taylor. *Teaching Reading in the Social Studies*. Newark, Delaware: International Reading Association, 1978.

Mikulecky, Larry, & Rita Haugh. *Reading in the Business Classroom*. Washington, D.C.: National Education Association, 1980.

Piercey, Dorothy. *Reading Activities in Content Areas: An Ideabook for Middle and Secondary Schools* (2nd ed.). Boston: Allyn & Bacon, 1982.

Robinson, H. Alan. *Teaching Reading and Study Strategies: The Content Areas* (2nd ed.). Boston: Allyn & Bacon, 1978.

Robinson, H. Alan, & Ellen Lamar Thomas. *Fusing Reading Skills and Content*. Newark, Delaware: International Reading Association, 1969.

Roe, Betty D., Barbara Stoodt, & Paul C. Burns. *Reading Instruction in the Secondary School* (2nd ed.). Boston: Houghton Mifflin, 1983.

Rubin, Dorothy. *Teaching Reading and Study Skills in Content Areas*. New York: Holt, Rinehart and Winston, 1983.

Shepherd, David L. *Comprehensive High School Reading Methods* (3rd ed.). Columbus, Ohio: Charles Merrill, 1982.

Singer, Harry, & Dan Donlan. *Reading and Learning from Text*. Boston: Little, Brown, 1980.

Smith, Cyrus F., & Henry S. Kepner. *Reading in the Mathematics Classroom*. Washington, D.C.: National Education Association, 1981.

Strang, Ruth, Constance M. McCullough, & Arthur E. Traxler. *The Improvement of Reading*. New York: McGraw-Hill, 1967.

Thelen, Judith. *Improving Reading in Science* (2nd ed.). Newark, Delaware: International Reading Association, 1984.

Thomas, Ellen L., & H. Alan Robinson. *Improving Reading in Every Class: A Sourcebook for Teachers* (3rd ed.). Boston: Allyn & Bacon, 1982.

Note: A chart showing *Books with Discussions on Specific Content Areas* is shown on page 116.

References

Criscuolo, Nicholas P., Richard T. Vacca, & Joseph L. LaVorgna. "What Reading Strategies Make Sense to Content Area Teachers," *Reading World*, 1980, *19*, 265-271.

Dewitz, Peter A., Mary Jo Henning, & Judythe P. Patberg. "The Effects of Content Area Reading Instruction on Teacher Behavior," in Judythe P. Patberg (Ed.), *Reading in the Content Areas: Application of a Concept*. Toledo, Ohio: University of Toledo, 1982.

Books with Discussions on Specific Content Areas

	Art	Business	Communication	English	Foreign Language	Home Economics	Industrial Arts	Mathematics	Music	Physical Education and Health	Science	Social Studies
Aukerman		X	X			XX*	X	X			X	XX
Bechtel & Franzblau											X	
Bristow & Farstrup										X		
Bullock & Hesse												X
Cowen	XX		X	X				XX				
Cunningham, Cunningham & Arthur			X	X				X			X	X
Duffy			X					X			X	X
Earle								XX				
Gentile										XX		
Graves, Palmer & Furniss			X									
Hafner	XX	X	XX	X	X		X	XX	XX	X	X	XX
Laffey			X					X			X	X
Lamberg & Lamb	X	X	X	XX	X		X	X	X	X	X	X
Lundstrum & Taylor												XX
Mikulecky & Haugh		XX										
Piercey	X	X	X	X	X	X	X	X	X	X	X	X
Robinson		X	X			X	X	X			X	X
Robinson & Thomas	X	X	X	X		X		X	X	X	X	X
Roe, Stoodt & Burns	X	X	X	X		X	X	X	X	X	X	X
Rubin								X			X	X
Shepherd	X	XX	X	X	X		X	XX	X	X	X	XX
Singer & Donlan			XX					X			X	X
Smith & Kepner								X				
Strang, McCullough & Traxler		X	XX	X	X	X	X	X			X	X
Thelen											X	
Thomas & Robinson	XX	XX		XX	XX	XX	XX	XX	XX	XX	XX	XX

* Two X's mean that the source gives particularly helpful suggestions.

Chapter Five

Selecting Presentation Methods and Staffing

Mary Dunn Siedow

Teachers have some definite preferences about inservice education
which have a bearing on the planning of inservice programs in
content area reading. Zirkel and Albert (1979) surveyed 288 elementary, middle, and high school teachers in twelve schools. They
determined that teachers are concerned about general elements of
inservice education. Teachers generally prefer workshops to conventions, especially when incentives (released time, renewal credit)
are available. They prefer learning about instructional strategies to
learning philosophy, and they list demonstrations, presentations,
and credit courses as their order of preference for format. They
consider experienced teachers to be good presenters and believe
that the most useful inservice is based on their perceived interests.

As they work to design and implement successful reading
inservice for content area teachers, coordinators should keep teacher preference in mind. They should begin by formulating objectives
which are appropriate for the needs of the teachers involved. They
should then plan content for sessions which meets the objectives
and which features instructional ideas and strategies likely to be
successful in content classrooms. Part of this planning of content is
the selection of presentation methods which will facilitate teachers'
learning of ideas and strategies. Another part of this planning is
identifying individuals who will most effectively present the ideas
and strategies to teachers. Although the planning of content, presentation methods, and staffing are considered separately in this
monograph, inservice coordinators are urged to remember that the
three are most effectively integrated when planned together.

The importance of selecting appropriate presentation methods is illustrated by Strother's account (1982) of using two different presentation methods during inservice to acquaint teachers with uses of microcomputers. In the first unsuccessful method, the presenter spent time individually introducing teachers to microcomputers. In the second method, the same presenter taught students to use software and soon had teachers willingly paying to attend extracurricular classes with students. In this case, use of hands–on experience to overcome initial trepidation was coupled with goal directed learning experiences. The resulting success was enjoyed by both teachers and students.

The presentation methods employed in inservice sessions are important for a variety of reasons. One very important reason is that adults learn differently from children. Methods employed to teach adults should be appropriate for their learning styles. Another reason is that inservice sessions are often conducted under adverse circumstances, during after school times when teachers are tired, in locations (such as workrooms or lounges) which are not conducive to learning; and with reluctant participants, occasionally including individuals who have been forced to attend. Under such conditions, it is easy to understand why inservice participants may become negative, and occasionally uncooperative. To win participants over to new points of view requires compelling presentations and energetic staffing. A third reason has to do with the levels of objectives discussed in Chapter 3. Objectives related to teacher beliefs may require different learning methods than do those related to teacher behaviors; those related to student behaviors and learnings may require still different methods.

In this chapter, we will examine the selection of presentation methods and staffing for content area inservice sessions. We will begin by discussing adult learning styles and the kinds of methods which are consistent with them. We will then suggest criteria for selecting methods likely to be successful for content area reading inservice. Finally, we will discuss staffing for inservice sessions which is consistent with the content and methods planned.

Teacher Developmental Levels

Adults learn differently from children; but, like children, they learn in ways which are parallel to their age and developmental levels. Bents and Howey (1981) reviewed research into adult learning and its impact on staff development. Young adults, for example, or those at lowest developmental levels, may look for and respect definite methods and the authority figures who propose them. At later developmental levels, individuals may question authoritative approaches and may want to explore alternatives rather than accepting one as definitive. Other adults may feel uneasy with definitive methods or alternative approaches and may decline to alter their practices for either. Adult development by age and by level are not necessarily synonymous, making it difficult to generalize about adult learning. Generalization should not be taken for granted, but should be examined in respect to each particular group of adults.

One means of viewing the professional development of teachers has been proposed by Yarger and Mertens (1980). They state that teachers move through six stages of development, and that the experiences of each contribute to their professional expertise. The first two stages, preeducation student and education student, are of concern in preservice education. The final four stages, beginning teacher (0-1 yr. experience); developing teacher (1-3 yrs. experience); practicing teacher (3-8 yrs. experience); and experienced teacher (8 yrs. experience), are of most relevant concern in inservice education, although experiences from preservice education also might be taken into account.

The beginning teacher and the developing teacher are both novices, still feeling their ways professionally, still accepting the authorities from preservice education and still searching for workable basic strategies and management techniques. Beginning and developing teachers want to learn the right way or the best way through inservice experiences.

The practicing teacher has become more stable and confident. Demonstrated ability to function in classrooms, high priority placed on content expertise, and growing awareness of professional roles characterize practicing teachers. Practicing teachers want to learn several alternatives and to expand themselves professionally through inservice experiences.

Finally, there are the experienced teachers. Individuals in this stage are characterized by a sense of security about their work which may lead to complacency. Whereas individuals in the three previous categories may see inservice as a means of learning and broadening, experienced teachers may see it as a means of reflecting and sharing.

Since teachers fitting each of these categories are likely to be included in any inservice audience, care must be taken to select strategies consistent with each. In discussion of a lesson format like the Directed Reading Activity (DRA), for example, a prototype DRA might be demonstrated for beginning and developing teachers. Practicing teachers could act as team leaders to search for variations like the Directed Reading-Thinking Activity (DR-TA) or the Guided Reading Procedure (GRP), and experienced teachers could be called upon to reflect on situations in which each is likely to be most effective. It is helpful for coordinators and presenters to know the makeup of a participant group ahead of time. This will allow selection of presentation methods consistent with the group and individual needs and may result in better incorporation of existing teacher expertise into inservice sessions.

Selecting Presentation Methods for Inservice Sessions

Methods selected for presentations in inservice sessions should meet several criteria. They should be consistent with adult learning styles, and should promote teacher effectiveness across any differences in content areas. A second criterion is that presentation methods should match the content and objectives identified for inservice in a manner which will promote content area classroom implementation of content learned in inservice. A third criterion is that presentation methods should overcome possible physical limitations of sessions and maintain consistency and interest across as well as within sessions.

The development of effective presentation methods for content area reading inservice should be consistent with adult learning styles described above and should promote teacher effectiveness across content areas. Knowles (1978, 1980) provides a set of principles which can be used to guide adult learning. He says that adult learning should be experiential, life-centered, and self directing in order to take advantage of the knowledge, experience, motivation, and independence which adults bring to the learning experience; and, at the same time, adult learning should be tolerant of the differences among people due to age and experience. Blair (1982) echoes some of these ideas as he discusses ways of promoting teacher efficacy and effort. Inservice, he says, will be more effective when it is based on an assumption of teacher potential rather than deficiency and on a recognition of the belief systems of teachers. The strategies taught will be best learned when they are backed by findings of teacher effectiveness studies; the presentation methods employed to teach these strategies will be most successful when they create dissatisfaction in teachers with their current strategies and present new strategies as sensible and positive alternatives. These latter points seem particularly appropriate for content area teachers.

Presentation methods should be designed to create a sense of dissatisfaction with current practice and to present sensible, positive alternatives for introducing vocabulary, preparing students for reading assignments, and conducting discussions. As they begin to understand the strategies presented, content area teachers are likely to be receptive to employing proposed alternatives in their classrooms.

Presentation methods for inservice sessions should be consistent with the objectives and content chosen for the sessions. When objectives concern teacher knowledge, content will be intellectually demanding and methods should facilitate the assimilation of ideas. Here a participatory demonstration of a DRA or GRP might be appropriate. Where alteration of teacher behavior is the objective, content will be lighter (possibly from sample student texts) and target strategies could be role played, then practiced for later classroom implementation.

The ultimate goal of any inservice session is that classroom implementation of strategies learned will produce desired changes in student behaviors and learning. There are some fairly consistent statements in the literature to the effect that the organization of sessions and inclusion of certain types of activities within them are likely to promote classroom applications once sessions are completed. Joyce and Showers (1980) identified five main components of training in successful inservice programs they reviewed: 1) presentation of theory or description of skill or strategy; 2) modeling or demonstration of skills or models of teaching; 3) practice in simulated or classroom settings; 4) structured and open-ended feedback; and 5) coaching for application and transfer of strategies to classroom. Rubeck (1978) reported that teachers she surveyed preferred sessions in which demonstrations were followed by descriptions and time for participants to plan and practice applications of techniques. Vacca and Vacca (1980) and Vacca (1981) suggest that a similar system serves to effect change in teachers by replacing existing practices with more effective strategies. Henning and Inglis (1982) report that sessions which include demonstrations and modeling, discussions of methods, and supervised practice with feedback are likely to result in implementation of methods learned by content area teachers.

Translating such observations to the organization of an inservice session yields a plan that in all likelihood will result in application of ideas presented to classroom practice. In such a plan, presentation methods are chosen to serve different functions throughout a session. Initial methods should serve as ice breakers, introducing participants and presenters to one another and to the content of the session. An example of an ice breaking method for people who do not know each other well might be for everyone to talk among themselves until they can fit into groups of three based on some random criteria (e.g., hair color, most similar hobbies, or most recently viewed movie). Other examples of icebreakers can be found in Vacca and Vacca (1980).

In addition to introducing participants to one another, initial activities should be motivational in nature. Brainstorming about changes teachers would like to make in their schools or departments helps participants see that problems and most obstacles to change are outside themselves. Discussions of strategies teachers would like to share could be used to illustrate participants' existing competence and future potential. A problem solving activity in which teachers discuss an instructional problem, suggest possible solutions, and share the one solution they believe is most appropriate with the entire group could be used to illustrate that participants have an understanding of their current situations and that their views about instruction are to be mutually respected throughout the inservice program. Ultimately, the initial presentation methods employed in inservice should draw content area teachers together, and should motivate both participants and presenters in preparation for individual sessions and for the entire inservice program.

Once the initial methods have succeeded in preparing participants for a session, attention can be turned to meeting the session's major objectives. In most sessions, objectives will come from all of the levels described in Chapter 3. This allows the training components outlined above to be used in combination, which Joyce and Showers (1980) affirm increases their effectiveness. For maximum impact, the training components might be organized into a sequence such as that described below.

The session might begin with a demonstration which provides firsthand experience with an instructional strategy. In such a demonstration the presenter would model the strategy using content related to the strategy so that participants could learn from the experience and the content. The demonstration could be followed by a discussion of the strategy, its theoretical foundation, and content area situations in which it is likely to be successful. Next, time could be provided for teachers to practice the method with simulation materials or content textbooks. Feedback from the presenter and from fellow participants could follow the practice and modifications could be made in the strategy. Finally, participating teachers could commit themselves to trying the method in their classrooms, and to reporting their experiences at succeeding sessions.

Any number of examples could be given of the sequence described above. Two examples are provided here. In a session dealing with vocabulary development strategies, the presenter might begin by demonstrating several strategies, then discuss common elements by which the strategies are related to concept learning. Practice feedback, and application activities could follow.

Figure 1. Sample session: Vocabulary development strategies.

To begin the vocabulary session, the presenter might introduce the strategies which will be used. Capsule Vocabulary (Crist, 1975) is a strategy in which 10-15 related terms are introduced, defined, practiced, and learned as an integrated set. List-Group-Label (Readence & Searfoss, 1981) is a strategy in which students list terms that pertain to a topic and then group and label related terms. Demonstrations of each strategy might follow the introduction.

Capsule Vocabulary
1. Introduce the ''capsule'' of 10-15 related terms by pronouncing each word and writing it on a blackboard. Participants write words in their notebooks.

2. Divide participants into pairs to review the words orally. Each participant is to use each word in context at least once.
3. Each participant writes a brief (one page) "composition" using as many of the capsule words as possible. These may be turned in or kept by participants. A few should be read aloud to reinforce the lesson.

List-Group-Label

1. *List.* Write the topic on the blackboard. Use an open question to elicit related terms.
   "What are some words that come to your mind when you think about trees?"
   Write all responses on the board.
2. *Group.* Ask participants to compose groups of related terms.
   "Which of these words can we put together because they are alike in some way?"
   Write the groups in lists.
3. *Label.* Ask participants to label the groups they have made.
   "What name can we give to this group that shows how the words are related?"
   Write the label above the group. Underline it.
   NB. Frequently participants will label groups as they develop them.
   When this happens, write the label above the group immediately.

Upon completion of the demonstrations, the strategies should be discussed. Both are aimed at the development of concepts; both rely on participants' experiences and prior knowledge; both provide opportunities to associate word meanings and to explore ways in which words can be related. The presenter might make the following suggestions for introducing content area vocabulary.

1. Be sure students hear the word correctly. Pronounce the word carefully in an appropriate context.
2. Be sure students understand the meaning of the word. Use concrete examples and examples which are within students' experiences.
3. Relate the new word to words students already know. Point out structural and conceptual similarities. Make associations among words that can be learned together.

4. Point out anything especially memorable about the word. Discuss word origins, familiar expressions which include the word, etc.

In the time allowed for practice, teachers might work with partners or in small groups to develop their own examples of the strategies. Completed examples should be shared, with participants offering constructive criticism to one another. The session should end with each teacher agreeing to try out one strategy and to report on the experience at the next inservice session.

In another session, this one designed to encourage teachers to develop question strategies leading to higher levels of comprehension, the presenter might ask a hierarchical sequence of questions based on a passage reviewing several studies on questioning. Participants could develop question sequences on content area assignments and practice them on one another for feedback and modification. Classroom applications would follow, with teachers observing one another to enhance their understanding of how such sequences work.

Figure 2. Sample session: Questioning strategies.

The presenter might begin the demonstration with a few words about questioning and then ask participants to read the following passage.

Research on Teacher Questioning Practices
by
David M. Memory

One of the most popular and significant subjects of educational research during the past fifty years has been teacher questioning practices. During that period hundreds of studies have been conducted and many important conclusions have been reached about the effects of questions on student learning. Some of those investigations have attempted to determine what types of questions are best suited for enhancing the learning of certain types of information. Other research has assessed the long term effects of the use of specific types of questions. A representative group of the studies on teacher questioning practices is described below.

In one such investigation Watts studied the use of literal questions. He had 96 sixth graders read 10 short passages about India. After each of the 10 passages, the 48 students in the experimental group read and answered a question about an important fact stated in the passage. The other students simply read the passages without questions. One week later all of the students were asked the 10 questions that the experimental group had seen during the reading of the passages. The students in the experimental group were able to answer 15 percent more of those literal questions than the students in the control group.

Birchall conducted a somewhat different study to assess the effects of inferential questions. He had 54 sixth graders read two SRA stories. While reading the stories, the 27 students in the experimental group came to 14 interspersed questions that required them to draw inferences from what they were reading. The other students read the stories, all of the students were asked the 14 inferential questions which the experimental group had already seen during the reading of the stories. The students in the experimental group answered 12 percent more of those questions than the students in the control group.

In a more complicated study Lucking was interested in the order in which questions were asked. As subjects, he used the twelfth graders taught by three beginning part-time English teachers. During the first week of the study, the teachers taught four short stories using the techniques they had learned in undergraduate English classes and on the fifth day had the students write an essay about one of those stories. Then during free time over a three day period, the teachers were given intensive training in the use of hierarchically-ordered questions. That is, they were taught to ask literal questions first, then inferential questions, and eventually higher level questions related to facts and inferences already discussed. Following the training, they worked together in planning hierarchically-arranged questions to use in teaching four other short stories. These stories and questions were then used with their classes during the next week of school, and the students again wrote an essay about one of the stories. Comparison of the essays written at the end of the first week with those written at the end of the final week of the study indicated that the students demonstrated more higher level thinking about the stories following the week of hierarchically-ordered questions than following the week of traditional discussions.

Hampton conducted a study designed to assess the effects of teacher use of higher level questions on student ability to answer questions of that type. In other words, she did not investigate whether higher level questions influence the understanding of and learning from the materials with which those questions are used. Instead, she was interested in whether the general ability to answer higher level questions improved. To examine that issue, she used six classes of fifth graders taught by three language arts teachers, with each one teaching an experimental class and a control class. For eight weeks the students in the experimental group were given an introductory overview and vocabulary assistance before each reading assignment and were provided with higher level questions to answer in writing about those assignments. During that period the students in the control classes followed the same procedures, except that factual questions were used rather than high level questions. During the ninth week of the experiment, all students took the Ohio State University Critical Reading Test. Analysis of results indicated that the experimental classes performed better than the control classes on the part of the test composed of the types of questions used earlier with the experimental classes.

Certainly none of these four studies is a definitive investigation of the effects of teacher questioning practices on student learning. Nevertheless, they do demonstrate that research in this area offers implications for teaching.

When participants have read the passage, the presenter might ask questions such as those which follow. The questions are arranged so that literal questions appear first followed by interpretive and applied questions. All are "open" questions, that is, they are designed to elicit multiple correct responses.

Literal Questions

To encourage a wide range of responses, the first question should be general and open.

"What are some things you read about questioning?"
Responses to the above question should be recorded, probably on a blackboard. If participants are reluctant or do not respond to all aspects of the passage, more focused questions should be asked. Again, answers should be recorded.

"What were the results of Watts' study?"

"What contributions did Lucking make to our knowledge of questioning?"

Interpretive Questions

Once literal information has been elicited, questions requiring inferences can be asked.

"What are some things we can infer from the information we've recalled?"

As inferences are made, the presenter can help participants relate them to facts by asking such questions as:

"On what basis can that inference be made?"

Should responses be slow in coming, more focused questions can be asked.

"What can be inferred about the effects of higher level questions on comprehension?"

"On what basis can that inference be made?"

Applied Questions

To complete the sequence, applied level questions can be used to make generalizations about the passage and its implications.

"Based on what you read and on our discussion, what general statements could we make about questioning in classrooms?

Upon completion of the demonstration, discussion centers on the sequence of questions used with the presenter pointing out the levels of questions and stressing that open questions are used throughout the sequence to allow several correct answers and thus encourage responses from many students. Concurrence between the sequence demonstrated and the research findings in the article can also be discussed. The sequence here is based on the work of Taba (1967) and could be used with any number of current articles on the subject of questioning. Participants may then use text passages to develop question sequences of their own. These can be tried out on one another with comments exchanged for improving the question sequences before they are used in classes.

The means of organizing a session just illustrated is consistent with the findings of authors cited earlier (Henning & Inglis, 1982; Rubeck, 1978; Vacca, 1981; Vacca & Vacca, 1980). It is also an organization which repeatedly has been found to be extremely successful in inservice presentations (Joyce & Showers, 1980). Participants are given an opportunity to see demonstrated an effective strategy which they are capable of implementing; they are encouraged to discover existing practices which might be replaced by it; and they are aided in developing, modifying, and evaluating their own applications of the strategy.

Inservice sessions following the demonstration, discussion, participation, feedback, and commitment format are particularly appropriate for learning about content area reading. At first glance, many strategies for content area reading are deceptively simple. Descriptions of study guides, DRA's, etc., seem logical and straightforward; actual preparation and application of these techniques can be complex and difficult. The session inservice format described above allows for growth in expertise with content area strategies over the time which may be needed for mastery and commitment to long term use.

Another consideration in selecting strategies for inservice sessions is that of the inservice situation itself. Sessions are often held after school when teachers are tired and would rather be grading papers or relaxing together before going home. Locating sessions in workrooms or media centers has the effect of inviting disruptions from nonparticipating teachers or students who want to use ditto machines or to locate books. While classrooms often are the best locations for inservice sessions, they still provide distractions due to the day's accumulations of papers, messy blackboards, and debris. Since the time and location of inservice sessions are often not conducive to effective learning, special care should be taken to select strategies which are imaginative and stimulating, both physically and mentally.

Patton and Anglin (1982) report that the negative effects of a room may be overcome when the activities selected for sessions work successfully. Activities requiring movement, manipulation of materials, and participant interaction should be interspersed with more reflective activities. In a session dealing with vocabulary reinforcement, for example, initial demonstrations requiring manipulations of word cards and lists might provide the initial motivation and lead into the discussion of a variety of strategies. In another session, this time dealing with study guides, participants might work in groups to complete a sample study guide for a text selection which provides a rationale for study guide use. After the guide has been completed and discussed, a reflective follow-up activity might be advantageous. Teachers could be given 3-5 minutes to engage in a free writing activity on the subject of study guide applications in their classrooms. This might provide just the stimulus needed to prepare teachers for developing study guides from their texts.

Use of strategies to demonstrate themselves (illustrated above) can be extremely effective as can group planning and role playing of strategies learned in inservice sessions. Ideally, sessions should end with commitments made by participants to try something learned in the session in their classrooms within a very short time, probably before the next inservice session.

The personal and professional characteristics of the participating content area teachers are an element of the inservice situation which also should be considered. The subject specialty differences that separate content area teachers have been discussed, as have the several levels of professional development at which teachers might be operating. No single inservice session can accommodate all of these differences. It may be beneficial to do some sessions by content area, with teachers from a single department meeting to implement a strategy introduced in a schoolwide session. Tables from Chapter 3 delineating specific needs of different content areas could guide the planning of these sessions. Here the nuances of applying a strategy to particular content can be worked out and appropriate attention can be paid to adaptations of procedures to fit content demands. Suggestions for successful adaptations can be found in the articles cited in the bibliography in Chapter 4. Here, also, the different stages of teacher development can be a positive force (Yarger & Mertens, 1980). Beginning and developing teachers can learn from experienced teachers. Experienced teachers can be renewed by sharing their accomplishments with professional teachers. Results of such sessions could well include enhanced departmental rapport in addition to increased teacher expertise.

A final criterion for selecting presentation methods for inservice sessions is to maintain consistency across sessions in a series. In arranging methods for presenting content and strategies among sessions, coordinators and presenters should consider that each individual session must have completeness within itself and also that each session should build on previous sessions and lead into the succeeding session. Some presentation methods can be used repeatedly, thus giving participants greater exposure to them and illustrating their versatility. In later sessions in a series, a portion of time might be set aside for discussion of classroom applications of content and strategies learned earlier. Teachers could learn from one another's successes and problems and instructional strategies. Presenters could use such times for troubleshooting, thus assuring optimal classroom applications of what has been learned in the inservice series.

Selecting Staff for Inservice Sessions

Staffing an inservice program for content area teachers requires dedication and industry on the part of the coordinator or inservice committee organizing and overseeing the series. The coordinator or committee would have a number of responsibilities throughout the inservice program. Its first task would be to conduct needs assessment and instill initial motivation. Next the committee or coordinator would plan the program, proposing objectives and selecting staff for individual sessions. Throughout the program the coordinator or committee would be responsible for maintaining the momentum and rapport of the series and for conducting interim needs assessment where necessary. Finally, the coordinator or committee would conduct evaluation and follow up activities.

In selecting staff for individual sessions of an inservice program, the coordinator or committee should, of course, keep in mind all elements of the proposed program. Presenters should be chosen as carefully as content and presentation methods; they should be people whose experience and qualifications make them willing and capable of meeting the objectives of the program.

There are several criteria which can be applied to the selection of presenters for sessions of an inservice program. Presenters should have expertise which complements the objectives and content chosen for sessions and should be capable of selecting presentation methods consistent with content. Presenters at sessions should be knowledgeable about adult learning styles; they should employ methods of presentation which are appealing to adults. Finally, presenters should be willing to commit their efforts both to their own sessions and to the entire inservice series.

Locating individuals who have expertise in content area reading and who can present that expertise to content teachers can be challenging. Coordinators and committee members should consider the full range of persons available. University faculty and state department consultants are obvious choices of individuals from outside school districts. Reading specialists and successful content area teachers from local or neighboring school districts can provide realistic and inspiring information based on their experiences. In some communities other individuals might also be available. Coordinators and committee members may conduct some inservice sessions themselves.

Once a list of possible presenters has been made, coordinators should carefully examine the capabilities of individuals being considered. University faculty selected should be people who are involved with content area reading instruction in their courses. State department consultants should be people who regularly work in content area classrooms. Local teachers should be those most capable of sharing their expertise with their peers.

The criterion of knowledge of adult learning styles is critical. Simply having a reputation as a good speaker or a successful teacher does not insure that an individual can teach adults. Vacca (1981) describes effective inservice presenters as individuals who were well prepared, who involved teachers as participants and who varied their methods of presentation. We have already discussed methods of presentation suitable for adults in inservice settings. Presenters at inservice sessions must be committed to employing such methods.

The final criterion, that of willingness to commit effort to the entire inservice program may be the most difficult to meet. It is contrary to the commonly accepted practice of "one shot" workshops which content area teachers have come to regard negatively. An inservice program which has unity across the sessions requires that the staff be present at planning sessions, visit classrooms of participants, and assist with all steps of the inservice model right through to follow up. University faculty, state department consultants, and local content area teachers may all be willing, even desirous of taking full roles in the inservice program, but their other responsibilities may prevent this. To prevent "one shot" situations from occurring, the number of outside presenters could be kept small; one or two individuals presenting several sessions are more likely to be willing to commit greater effort over longer times. Once again it is the responsibility of the inservice coordinator or committee to determine just what commitments will be required of each individual and to schedule these commitments so that the greatest benefit can accrue to participants.

Staffing of inservice sessions in content area reading is likely to be most successful when presenters represent varied expertise and when their roles in the total program are differentiated according to their expertise. Content area and reading teachers from within the district can be expected to have the most immediate understanding of local needs. These individuals might play major roles in needs assessment and follow up as well as making presentations at sessions. They might be asked to join coordinators and committees for the full range of planning and evaluation activities. Outside consultants have commitments to their own institutions. They may be able to play major roles in session presentations but only minor roles in follow-up activities. They might train teachers from the local district who will, in turn, conduct actual sessions.

Any differentiation will require cooperative efforts to presenters and inservice committees. It is likely that meetings of coordinators, committees, and presenters will have to be held. The emphasis at these meetings should be on assuring continuity across sessions by meeting stated objectives within sessions. Presenters should be furnished with an overview of the entire program, including objectives and content for sessions so they can plan their sessions to meet objectives and to complement others.

In Conclusion

The presentation methods selected for teaching instructional strategies in inservice session on content area reading are most likely to be successful when they meet criteria described in this chapter. Presentation methods should be appropriate for the learning styles of adults and for the promotion of effective content area teaching. They should be carefully matched to the content and objectives of sessions and adaptable to different content areas. Finally, they should be helpful in overcoming physical limitations of inservice locations and they should allow consistency across sessions in the inservice program.

Staffing for inservice programs should be varied to include local and outside presenters for sessions. Presenters should have experiences which complement the objectives, content, and strategies chosen for sessions. They should be capable of implementing presentation methods which are consistent with adult learning styles. They should also be willing to commit themselves to the total inservice program of which their sessions are part.

Successful inservice sessions are those in which the content, strategies, presentation methods, and staffing are planned together to meet objectives determined through needs assessment. A carefully integrated approach such as this will provide a substantial basis for the program and internal consistency across its sessions.

References

Bents, Richard H., & Kenneth R. Howey. "Staff Development-Change in the Individual," in Dillon-Peterson (Ed.), *Staff Development/Organization Development*. Alexandria: Association for Supervision and Curriculum Development, 1981, 11-36.

Birchall, Lester H. "An Investigation of the Main and Interaction Effects of Three Dimensions of Adjunct Questions upon the Performance of Sixth Grade Students on a Criterion Measure Consisting of Two Criteria—Literal Level and Interpretation Level Questions," doctoral dissertation, University of Maryland, 1975. *Dissertation Abstracts International*, 1976, *36*, 6455A-6456A.

Blair, Timothy. "Implementation of Reading Teacher Effectiveness Research Findings: Developing Inservice Training Models," presentation at National Reading Conference, Clearwater Beach, Florida, December 1982.

Crist, Barbara I. "One Capsule a Week—A Painless Remedy for Vocabulary Ills," *Journal of Reading*, 1975, *19*, 147-149.

Earle, Richard A., & R. F. Barron. "An Approach for Teaching Vocabulary in Content Subjects," in Herber & Barron (Eds.), *Research in Reading in the Content Areas: Second Year Report*. Syracuse, New York: Syracuse University Reading and Language Arts Center, 1973, 84-100.

Hampton, Judith A. D. "The Effect of Elaborative Type Questions on Comprehension and Critical Reading Ability," doctoral dissertation, University of Missouri, 1972. *Dissertation Abstracts International*, 1973, *34*, 2459A-2460A.

Henning, Mary Jo, & Joan D. Inglis. "Inservice Teachers in Reading in the Content Areas: From Theory to Practice," in J. P. Patberg (Ed.), *Reading in the Content Areas: Application of a Concept*. Toledo, Ohio: University of Toledo, 1982, 90-99.

Joyce, Bruce, & Beverly Showers. "Improving Inservice Training: The Messages of Research," *Educational Leadership*, 1980, *37*, 379-385.

Knowles, Malcolm S. *The Adult Learner: A Neglected Species*. Houston: Gulf Publishing, 1978.

Knowles, Malcolm S. *The Modern Practice of Adult Education*. Chicago: Follett, 1980.

Lucking, Robert A. "A Study of the Effects of a Hierarchically-Ordered Questioning Technique on Adolescents' Responses to Short Stories," *Research in the Teaching of English*, 1976, *10*, 269-276.

Patton, William E., and Leo W. Anglin. "Characteristics of Success in High School Inservice Education," *High School Journal*, 1982, *65*, 163–168.

Readence, John E., & Lyndon W. Searfoss. "Teaching Strategies for Vocabulary Development," in Dishner, Bean, & Readence (Eds.), *Reading in the Content Areas: Improving Classroom Instruction*. Dubuque, Iowa: Kendall/Hunt, 1981, 148-152.

Rubeck, Patricia. "How to Conduct Effective Inservice Programs," *Reading Improvement*, 1978, *15*, 170-171.

Strother, Deborah Burnett. "Microcomputers in Education: Two Inservice Experiences," *Practical Applications of Research*, 1982, *4*, 1.

Taba, Hilda. *Teachers' Handbook for Elementary Social Studies*, Reading, Massachusetts: Addison-Wesley, 1967.

Vacca, Jo Anne L. "Working with Content Area Teachers," in Vacca, *Content Area Reading*. Boston: Little, Brown, 1981, 305–329.

Vacca, Jo Anne L., & Richard T. Vacca. "Unfreezing Strategies for Staff Development in Reading," *Reading Teacher*, 1980, *34*, 27-31.

Watts, Graeme H. "The Effect of Adjunct Questions on Learning from Written Instruction by Students from Different Achievement Levels," *Australian Journal of Education*, 1975, *19*, 78-87.

Yarger, S. J., & S. K. Mertens. "Testing the Waters of School Based Teacher Education," in Corrigan & Howey (Eds.), *Concepts to Guide the Teaching of Teachers*. Reston, Virginia: Council for Exceptional Children, 1980.

Zirkel, Perry A., and Victoria F. Albert. "Assessing Teachers' Preferences Regarding Inservice Education," *The Clearinghouse*, 1979, *52*, 328–333.

Chapter Six

Evaluating Inservice Effectiveness

Page S. Bristow

Evaluation is a particularly important facet of content area reading inservice. Content area teachers often enter the inservice process with some skepticism and less than optimal motivation. Therefore, evaluation can play a vitally important role in encouraging and motivating teachers through monitoring and demonstrating participants' growth in knowledge and skill; monitoring and demonstrating their students' growth as strategies are implemented; and displaying, to administrators and the general public, teachers' and students' accomplishments. The role of evaluation as ongoing needs assessment is also crucially important in content area reading inservice. Since content area teachers have particularly varied needs due to the diversity of their content areas and since many teachers show rather marked attitude changes as the inservice progresses, ongoing evaluation is quite important. Only through careful monitoring of teachers' accomplishments and needs can the inservice provide for maximum learning and motivation.

Evaluation activities can be broadly classified into two types: product evaluation, which measures accomplishment of program objectives; and process evaluation which attempts to explain why the expected objectives were or were not met. For example, assume one objective was "after inservice education teachers will be able to manage the use of the multilevel textbooks." If so, one purpose of evaluation would be to determine whether teachers actually were able to manage the use of multilevel textbooks. This objective might be measured through teacher interviews, observations, or teacher questionnaires. Measurement of this objective is an example of product evaluation.

In the example above, evaluation would determine whether teachers were able to manage multilevel textbooks; however, process evaluation would help explain why the objectives were met or if they were not, why not. If through an interview we found that multilevel texts were not being used, process evaluation would consist of questions probing *why* the texts were not being used. Teacher responses might indicate that the multilevel texts available did not match the reading levels of students in the class, or perhaps, that the multilevel texts had contained nonparallel information and the teacher was unable to handle the divergence. This process information is vitally important in providing ongoing needs assessment, indicating when modifications are needed.

Process evaluation is usually conducted through perceptions questionnaires, interviews and/or observations. Inservice session process factors frequently assessed include participant perceptions of content appropriateness, effectiveness of methods of presentations, organization, atmosphere, setting, quality of presentations, and usefulness of information presented. Process factors which may be assessed during or after follow-up assistance include: participants', administrators' and/or students' perceptions of the usefulness of techniques implemented; ease of implementing techniques; quality of follow-up assistance; availability of follow-up assistance; and appropriateness of its frequency.

As stated earlier, product evaluation involves measuring whether inservice objectives have been met. Categorizing the objectives according to the levels described in Chapter 3 can simplify the selection of evaluation techniques. Since the levels of objectives relate to specific types of teacher or student characteristics, classification allows us to focus on particular evaluation methods which are most appropriate for measuring these characteristics. For example, if an objective is on the level of teacher beliefs, then the most appropriate way to measure those beliefs may be through a questionnaire such as the Vaughan Attitude Scale described in Chapter 2. Responses to this questionnaire, administered after the inservice, could be compared to responses to the same questions previously measured on the needs assessment questionnaire. Positive changes in beliefs would indicate that the objective had been met. Table 1 contains a listing of the levels of objectives outlined in Chapter 3. For each objective type, methods which are most appropriate for measuring these objective types are listed.

Table 1
Methods for Evaluating Various Objective Types

Objective Types	Evaluation Methods
Teacher Beliefs	Pre/Post: questionnaires 　　　　interviews 　　　　observations 　　　　review of lesson plans
Teacher Abilities	Observations/videotapes Self-assessment quizzes Pre/Post: questionnaires 　　　　interviews 　　　　observations 　　　　review of lesson plans
Teacher Practices	Record of activities Lesson plan reviews Observations/videotapes Interviews Questionnaires
Student Behaviors	Student interviews Student questionnaires Teacher logs Observation Teacher interviews
Student Learnings	Chapter/unit tests Standardized test Teacher logs Student assignments Comparison of present term grades to 　　previous grades (or grades of another 　　group of students) Student interviews Teacher questionnaires Student questionnaires Teacher interviews

Developing an Evaluation Plan

Ideally, coordinators should develop their inservice evaluation plan as they plan their objectives. Designing an evaluation plan can be an excellent way to check the clarity and feasibility of the objectives which have been selected. Objectives which are difficult or impossible to evaluate usually are also inappropriate. If success cannot be measured in any clear way, then it will be extremely difficult to be sure that the inservice has had any real value. It would be much more satisfying for all involved to select objectives that are realistic, obtainable, and measurable so that success can be validated through the evaluation plan. Virtually any viable objective that is clearly attainable is also measurable in some way. Many ideas for measurement of objectives and factors that affect their attainment will be provided in the sections which follow.

A number of factors must be considered when developing an evaluation plan. First, it is helpful to classify objectives according to type (i.e. teacher beliefs, teacher ability). Next, the methods of evaluating the objectives must be selected. Table 1 provides suggestions of measurement methods that might be used; these methods are also discussed in some detail later in this chapter. Finally, a timetable of evaluation activities should be developed. Without this timetable, evaluation points may be overlooked or evaluation instruments may not be prepared in time for use.

The complexity of an evaluation plan should be directly related to the complexity of inservice objectives, the duration of the inservice, and the intensity of the effort. While evaluation of a "one shot inservice" would probably consist of a short questionnaire administered at the end of the inservice session, an extended inservice series which includes a follow-up component will certainly warrant a more extensive evaluation plan.

Timetable Development

The decision of when to evaluate is made easily if the inservice is of short duration with no follow-up assistance provided. However, timing of evaluation efforts for a more extensive series becomes more complicated and can prove quite important. If a series of inservice sessions includes a follow-up component, evaluation activities will probably be scheduled for at least three points in time. If any inservice series contains four or more sessions, workshop planners will probably plan the first evaluation point either after the first few sessions or halfway through the inservice series. Their purpose at that point will be to monitor participants' reactions to the sessions and to identify process factors that could be improved to increase the effectiveness of the series. A second point where evaluation activities usually occur is at the completion of the formal inservice series. At this point product objectives related to teacher beliefs and teacher ability are usually measured as is process evaluation related to session activities. Evaluation activities also may provide an opportunity to determine follow-up needs.

If objectives in teacher practices and student behaviors and learnings are included, evaluation of these objectives may not be possible until three to nine months following the end of formal inservice activities. Changes in student learnings may not be measurable until quite some time after formal activities have ended, especially if standardized instruments are used for measurement. The firm establishment of new teacher practices also may not be evident until months after the formal inservice series ends.

Table 2 (see pages 142-143) contains an example of a rather extensive evaluation plan designed to measure objectives for a six session inservice series which includes follow-up assistance to be provided periodically for at least six months thereafter. It should be noted that evaluation methods are listed for each objective separately; however, in many cases they are redundant. For example, the teacher perceptions questionnaire referred to in evaluation of objectives Ia, Ib, Id, and Ie would be only one questionnaire which would contain individual questions measuring each of the objectives separately.

Development of Evaluation Questionnaires

Of the methods of evaluation listed in Tables 1 and 2, the questionnaire is probably the most widely used. Its wide use justifies special consideration here since the effectiveness of the questionnaire development may have a significant effect on the overall quality of the evaluation.

Item Formats

A number of different formats may be used for items on an evaluation questionnaire. These formats are generally categorized into two types: forced-choice, closed-response items; and open-response items. Each type has its advantages and disadvantages.

Forced-choice, closed-response items include: multiple choice statements with which participants agree or disagree, checklist responses, Likert scale items, and semantic differentials. Examples of each kind of item are shown in Figures 1-5.

Figure 1. Sample from an evaluation questionnaire (multiple choice).

How much do you feel you've learned from this content reading inservice?
     a. a great deal
     b. a fair amount
     c. very little
     d. nothing

Figure 2. Sample from an evaluation questionnaire (statements).
Below are listed a number of statements. If you agree with the statement, put an A in the space provided; if you disagree, put a D in the space. ___1. Content teachers should take responsibility for teaching students strategies that will help them master the concept–carrying vocabulary specific to their content areas. ___2. Content area teachers should take responsibility for teaching the basic reading skills if their students have not already acquired them.

Figure 3. Sample excerpt from an evaluation questionnaire (checklist).

Put a check beside the techniques that you fully expect to implement in your classroom.
  ___ systematic vocabulary instruction   ___ structured overviews
  ___ multilevel study guides   ___ the Unit approach
  ___ SQ3R   ___ use of multilevel tests

Figure 4. Sample excerpt from an evaluation questionnaire (Likert scale item).					
	Excellent				*Poor*
The overall quality of the inservice sessions was:	5	4	3	2	1

Table 2
Example of an Evaluation Plan

Objectives	Objective Type	Method of Evaluation	Time Table
1. After participation in a series of six inservice sessions, a greater percentage of teachers will:*			
a. Believe that they have a responsibility to teach students strategies that will help them handle the printed materials used in content classrooms	Teacher Beliefs	Questionnaire	Last inservice session
b. Understand how to use multilevel texts in the classroom	Teacher Ability	Self-assessment quiz Teacher perceptions questionnaire	Last inservice session
c. Be able to compute text readability using the Fry Readability Graph	Teacher Ability	Teacher's worksheet	Workshop session #2
d. Be able to use at least 3 techniques for preteaching technical vocabulary in their content areas	Teacher Ability	Workshop product Teacher perceptions questionnaire	Workshop session #4
e. Be able to design a preteaching guide for material from the major text used in the content classroom	Teacher Ability	Workshop product (preteaching guide) Teacher perceptions questionnaire	Workshop session #5 Last inservice session
2. After follow-up activities, at least 50 percent of the inservice participants will:			
a. Regularly use multilevel texts in at least one of their classes	Teacher Practices	Questionnaire Observation	6 months after last inservice session 3 months after last inservice session
b. Regularly preteach technical vocabulary to students in at least one of their classes	Teacher Practices	Teacher lesson plans questionnaire	Check monthly for 6 months after inservice session
c. Have computed readability formulas on the major content text used in their classroom	Teacher Practices	Readability worksheet submitted to inservice coordinator	1 month after last inservice session

Objective	Category	Evaluation Instrument	Timeline
d. Regularly use prereading guides with at least a portion of their students in at least one class	Teacher Practices	Teacher lesson plans questionnaire	Check monthly for 6 months after inservice session
3. After their teachers participate in the inservice series and follow-up activities students will:			
a. Show increased willingness to do assigned readings and exercises	Student Behaviors	Review of teacher grade book (increase in student assignments completed)	1–6 months after implementing strategies
		Student perceptions questionnaire	2 weeks to 6 months after implementing strategies
b. Demonstrate increased comprehension of content materials	Student Learnings	Chapter or unit tests	2–6 months after implementing techniques
		Grades on homework assignments	2–6 months after implementing techniques
c. Demonstrate increased knowledge of technical vocabulary	Student Learnings	Chapter or unit tests	2–6 months after implementing techniques
		Vocabulary tests	1–6 months after implementing techniques
d. Demonstrate overall improvement in content area learning	Student Learnings	Student grade reports	3–9 months after implementing techniques
		Standardized tests	6 months to 1 year after implementing techniques
		Student perceptions questionnaire	2–8 months after implementing techniques

* Since this objective stem says "a greater percentage of teachers will," it will be necessary to compare these results to preservice information collected during the needs assessment phase of planning. A comparison with student data prior to the inservice also will be necessary to measure student progress.

Figure 5. Sample excerpt from an evaluation questionnaire (semantic differential).
In the semantic differentials below, please check the blank that illustrates your evaluation of this inservice session.
interesting — — — — — boring effective — — — — — ineffective practical — — — — — impractical

Forced-choice, closed-response items have several advantages. They are relatively simple to summarize and report, especially when the number of participants to be surveyed is large. They specifically focus participants on topics which the evaluators feel are important. They may provide more comprehensive coverage of the topics to be evaluated. They also require relatively little response time. Closed-response items also have some disadvantages. While items of this type may very well focus the participant on the evaluator's concerns, they may not allow participants to address issues which they feel are important. Forced-choice items must be written carefully with clear directions, otherwise they can be confusing to participants.

Open-ended response items ask participants to respond in phrases, sentences, or paragraphs. Figure 6 displays an example of open-ended questions.

Figure 6. Sample excerpt from an evaluation questionnaire (open-ended question).
1. What aspect of this workshop series did you find most helpful?
2. If this workshop were to be offered again, what should be changed, added, or deleted?

Open-ended response items have several advantages. If phrased properly, they give participants a chance to more openly express their responses to the workshop. The opportunity to elaborate often provides much more insight to inservice planners regarding why objectives were met (or why they were not). Open-ended responses also give an opportunity for the participants to make constructive suggestions or clearly express their needs. Frequently they make statements that might not have been anticipated by the evaluators.

There are some negative aspects to open-ended response items. Results are much more time consuming to summarize and sometimes difficult to group into summary statements. These items do not usually provide as comprehensive an evaluation as do closed-response items. While dependent on the number of questions included, the open-response questionnaire is usually much more time consuming to complete than the closed-response questionnaire. Participants must have a somewhat higher level of commitment to thoroughly, thoughtfully complete an open-response questionnaire. If they have a lesser commitment, they may either return questionnaires partially completed, or not return them at all.

The item format selected for questionnaires should be based on a number of considerations: number of participants responding, type of information needed, ways the results will be used, amount of time respondents can be expected to spend on the questionnaire, and amount of time evaluators have to spend summarizing and analyzing results. Evaluators may want to use a combination of open and closed format items to strike a balance among the various factors relevant to an individual situation.

Factors Influencing the Effectiveness of a Questionnaire

A number of other factors influence the effectiveness of a questionnaire. Some of these are:

1. *Length.* Generally, questionnaires should be no longer than two pages unless respondents have extraordinary commitment to their completion. If the questionnaire is designed to measure an inservice program of very limited scope, the questionnaire should be made even shorter. When questionnaires are longer than one or two pages, participants generally complete them with less care, skip questions, or fail to complete them at all.

2. *Types of questions/answers incorporated.* As noted above, the type of questions used and answers requested can have a large effect on the quality of response, as well as the ease of summarizing results.

3. *Clarity of questions.* Questions which are vague or ambiguous are likely to result in inaccurate responses or no responses at all. Respondents are rarely willing to ask many clarifying questions and may just skip questions they don't understand.

4. *Organization.* Questions which relate to each other in content or question type should generally be grouped together.

5. *Adequacy of directions.* Directions should be clear, concise, and as simple as possible. Be sure respondents are certain what to do. For example, if respondents are asked to use a five-point scale, make sure they know whether a five is a very positive or a very negative response.

6. *Language.* Be sure the language complexity and sophistication are appropriate for the audience. Avoid the use of technical language that is not commonly understood by the respondents. When in doubt, simplify.

7. *Timing.* Distribution of a questionnaire to teachers when grades are due, or at 5 p.m. after the inservice session, are examples of poor timing and will almost certainly yield less than satisfactory results. Some time should be allowed to complete the questionnaire during the confines of the inservice session itself. Generally participants resent having to stay five or ten minutes after an inservice session to complete an evaluation questionnaire. Asking participants to take the evaluation with them and return it later may result in negative attitudes, hasty responses, or less than full return of the questionnaires. If the evaluation activity is worth doing, then it is worth taking a few minutes of the inservice time to administer it, insuring thoughtful responses and complete returns.

8. *Format.* Using a variety of question types and directions may prove confusing to respondents. Simplicity is generally the best policy. Crowded questions with too little space for thoughtful answers may prove frustrating to respondents.

Consideration of the factors listed above will certainly not ensure accurate, valid, questionnaire results; however, it may increase substantially the level of thoughtful response by participants.

Other Evaluation Methods

1. *Self-assessment quizzes.* Clearly, the best way to measure teacher knowledge/ability is to test it in some way. However, testing adults can be an uncomfortable process especially when inservice coordinators (who may be teachers' peers) are testing their colleagues. A self-assessment quiz is one way to ease this discomfort. Self-assessment quizzes are "corrected" by teachers themselves using answer sheets or by reviewing workshop materials. The self-assessment quiz enables teachers to objectively determine their own level of knowledge or ability.

2. *Observations.* Observations can be an excellent evaluation technique, providing process information as well as product information. Observations can be made substantially more productive, however, if some planning occurs prior to the observations. First the evaluators should decide what their purposes are for the observation. Next, evaluators should set up observation checklists or lists of questions to remind them to look for specifics during the observation. For example, if the purpose of an observation is to look for student behaviors that provide information regarding the effectiveness of techniques being implemented, the checklist might contain a list of behaviors that one would expect to see. Some behaviors listed would be indicative of behaviors expected if the techniques were less than successful. With the observer's behavior focused in this way, the observations are likely to be more systematic and more useful in evaluating the particular objectives set. In some other cases, however, observations are conducted to gather general process information. In this case, observing with no preconceived plan may be the most effective method. The purpose of the observation should dictate the structure imposed upon it.

3. *Chapter or unit test review.* A review of student test scores both before and after implementation of strategies designed to improve content reading abilities may show hard evidence that increased student learning has occurred. If students' unit test grades are better as a group than either their grades on previous unit tests or the grades of classes in years past, then the likelihood is good that improvement is due to the new strategies. As a more stringent test, teachers may want to select two sections of a course in which students in both sections have done comparable work. Then teachers may use the new techniques in one class while the regular

lessons are taught in the other class. A comparison of the groups' chapter or unit test scores could be a pretty good indication of the success of the program. This evaluation technique is often referred to as "action research." For further information about action research see Borg (1981).

4. *Student grade reports.* Student grade report comparisons can be made in much the same way as comparisons of chapter/unit tests suggested above. Teachers should keep in mind, however, that the usefulness of strategies will have to be much more powerful to affect a 6 or 9 week grade report. Many factors in addition to the effectiveness of the new techniques will contribute to students' term or semester grades. Statements in perceptions questionnaires from teachers, and/or students can be useful in confirming the role of the new techniques in student grade improvement.

5. *Standardized tests.* Commonly used to measure students' relative level of content area knowledge, standardized norm-referenced tests are another possible evaluation measure of inservice objectives. Chapter 2 mentions a number of commonly used standardized tests which can be employed for both needs assessment and evaluation of the effect of inservice. If they are used, however, evaluators must remember that standardized tests are a good measure of student learnings *only* when there is a very good match between the content area curriculum and the test content. This match is a vital prerequisite if inservice objectives are to be measured by standardized tests. Also, inservice planners must be sure that the scope of the inservice is robust enough to justify expectations of changes in standardized test scores. Otherwise, the inservice may result in real increases in student learnings but increases that are not robust enough to be measured on a standardized test.

Sometimes standardized tests are able to provide more specific information on student learnings than a general overall score, such as a percentile in social studies or science. Recently many of the commonly used standardized tests have begun to include objective referenced item scores in categories like "use of dictionary skills" or "technical vocabulary." If these objective related subscores match inservice objectives, and if the course curriculum matches the test content, use of a standardized test to measure these items may be a good evaluation technique. In many cases, however, it is not worth the time or money to administer a standardized test solely as a measure of the effect of inservice education. However, if the test is being given anyway, inservice planners may want to seriously consider using the results for evaluation purposes, with consideration of the limitations stated previously.

Summarizing, Analyzing, and Reporting Evaluation Results

A good evaluation plan formulated along with program objectives is the best way to reduce difficulty in summarizing, analyzing, and reporting results. If evaluation measures are carefully chosen and constructed with a clear view of the inservice objectives, then analysis, summarization, and reporting are usually relatively simple.

The reasons for evaluating the inservice program should be foremost in ones' mind as findings are summarized and reported. Showing whether the objectives of the inservice have been accomplished is probably one of the major purposes of the evaluation. Making the successes known to others (participants, administrators, students) is probably equally important. Use of the results of the evaluation in ongoing needs assessment to provide important information about program strengths, weaknesses, and further needs is also an important goal. All of these goals, along with others evaluators identify, should be addressed as the report is created.

Evaluation reports vary widely in comprehensiveness and sophistication, depending on the audience and the purpose of the evaluation report. If the audience is the school board or central office administrators, and the purpose is to justify a relatively large expenditure for continuation of a multiyear inservice program, then the evaluation report should be polished and complete. If the evaluation summary is to be used only by program participants for making program modifications, the report may be composed only of tallying responses on a blank copy of the questionnaire. Several resources for summarizing, analyzing, and reporting evaluation results exist (Patton, 1982; Popham, 1974; Rothman, 1980), therefore, detailed instructions are not provided here. However, a few general recommendations may provide some assistance.

1. The report should address directly the inservice objectives, stating whether they were met. Information from several sources should be synthesized to make a final judgment regarding each objective.

2. The report should include major highlights of findings, both product and process.

3. The audience for the evaluation report should be constantly remembered. The language, level of specificity, complexity, sophistication, methods of presenting data, and length all should be varied based on the audience being addressed. A report prepared for parents will be quite different from one prepared for reading by the program participants.

4. The purpose(s) of the evaluation also should be constantly kept in mind. Be sure that the information needed for these purposes is provided.

5. The report should be concise and clear. If the results are to be used, they must be understood. Keep the report as brief as possible while still providing the necessary information. It is not necessary to report all the information collected if it is irrelevant to the purposes of the report.

Using the Evaluation Results

If evaluation results are to have any value at all, they must be *used*. They may be used in any number of ways: 1) to measure success or failure in meeting inservice objectives; 2) to determine *why* inservice objectives were (or were not) met; 3) to justify continued allocation of resources to the inservice effort; 4) to provide evidence to teachers, administrators, students, and parents of the usefulness of the inservice; 5) to provide information that can be used to modify and improve the program; and 6) to provide information regarding follow-up assistance needed by teachers.

Evaluation and Needs Assessment: Close Parallels

The reader already may have noticed the close parallels between evaluation and needs assessment. In fact, evaluation and needs assessment are two sides of the same coin. Clearly, many of the techniques used are similar, if not identical. The relationship among evaluation, needs assessment, and well-developed objectives is a tight one; the needs assessment defines the objectives needed while the evaluation determines whether the original needs have been met. Evaluation may also serve as ongoing needs assessment, monitoring progress and noting modifications needed to ultimately

Bristow

meet the needs of participants and their students. Evaluation additionally serves as needs assessment in clarifying the follow-up assistance which should be provided to teachers following the formal inservice series. Chapter 7 will discuss this follow-up assistance in detail.

References

Borg, W.R. *Applying Educational Research: A Practical Guide for Teachers*. New York: Longman, 1981.

Patton, M.Q. *Practical Evaluation*. Beverly Hills, California: Sage, 1982.

Popham, W.J. (Ed.). *Evaluation in Education: Current Applications*. Berkeley, California: McCutchan, 1974.

Rothman, J. *Using Research in Organizations: A Guide to Successful Application*. Beverly Hills, California: Sage, 1980.

Chapter Seven

Providing Follow-Up Assistance

Page S. Bristow

A week or two after a content reading inservice series ends, a number of comments are commonly heard from inservice participants:

"The strategies described in the inservice session looked like a great idea at the time but now, two weeks later, I'm back in my classroom alone and I'm not sure what to do."

"Procrastination has set in; I *know* they are good ideas, but somehow it's easier to keep doing what I've done all along."

"The work load of making the changes discussed makes me reluctant to start. What if the changes work, and work well? Then I'll feel like I have to make these changes throughout the curriculum. How will I do it all?"

"What if I get started and don't know what to do? Or what if I try the strategies and they don't work well? Or what if students complain about extra work, and the changes? The students are used to the way things work now and while some aren't making good progress, things are running smoothly and I'm not sure I want to rock the boat."

Most professionals have had the experience of going to an inservice session, a workshop, or even a conference that is extremely motivating and exciting. All sorts of plans are made for ways to use what was learned; however, upon returning to work, all sorts of obstacles interfere with implementing these changes.

Major Obstacles to Strategy Implementation

Some of the major obstacles content area teachers have reported when considering implementing content reading strategies presented in inservice sessions are:

1. The size of the task (if they are committed to fully implementing a technique throughout the curriculum).
2. Difficulty applying the strategy presented once they are back in their own classrooms with their own materials and students.
3. Making the transition from teacher knowledge to teacher practice: developing new habits.
4. Coping with change, tolerating some failures, and making modifications until the strategy works well.

Follow-up assistance of various types can provide invaluable support when these problems are encountered. Discussions of each of these problems and some follow-up methods which can prove useful are provided below.

Size of Task

When teachers learn about strategies like using reading guides they are often quite enthusiastic. However, their enthusiasm is often quickly dampened by the realization that applying these techniques as needed throughout their curriculum can be a time consuming task.

A number of follow-up activities can make the job more manageable, however. First, consider having teachers share the work, either within a school or possibly districtwide. If several teachers teach the same content material out of the same text, they could get together, divide chapters and each do reading guides for a portion of the material. Then they could edit one another's work and have a higher quality product than if they had duplicated efforts working individually.

Second, encourage teachers to set priorities. They must focus their energies on the activities that will provide maximum benefit for minimum work. They might concentrate their efforts on units which have proved particularly troublesome for students and save units that presently work well for later efforts.

Third, encourage teachers to set a timeline for themselves, rather than expect to immediately implement all ideas presented. Other demands on teacher time also need to be considered. It may be necessary to set long range plans, perhaps over a year or more, for ambitious projects.

Fourth, remind teachers that doing something for the first time always takes longer than any time thereafter. They are certain to become much more time efficient with practice. For example, doing a Fry Readability Graph (Fry, 1977) on a text usually takes 15-20 minutes the first time, but after several tries teachers can usually cut the time down to 5-7 minutes.

Inability/Difficulty Applying the New Knowledge to Present Situation

During the inservice teachers have probably had opportunities to see examples of the strategies taught; in fact, they may also have been given an opportunity to begin applying the strategies to materials that they use in the classroom. However, after the support of the inservice sessions is over, teachers often have difficulty completing application of the idea. Some teachers may encounter a problem or get to a new part of the strategy and not know what to do. Other teachers may apply the strategy, find that it did not work quite as they had expected, and not know what to do next.

A number of follow-up methods can ease this difficulty. Coordinators should select from the methods below based on the level of support needed by participating teachers.

1. *Individual/Group Meetings.* The person designated to conduct follow up with teachers meets individually or in a group with teachers to identify follow-up needs, using the evaluation information collected from participants. All teachers who show a real interest in implementing ideas should be included, not just the people who anticipate problems. Teachers who are able to apply the strategies right away can serve as models for others.

2. *Peer Teams or Support Groups.* Once participants interested in working together to apply the strategies are identified, they may be divided into pairs or team support groups. These support groups or teams may meet periodically to discuss their progress in implementing strategies and may edit/critique others' applications of strategies. They also may observe in each other's classrooms, later discussing strong and weak points of the application.

3. *Demonstrations.* If demonstrations have not been included in the inservice sessions, teachers often find it helpful to actually see the techniques used with students (preferably theirs) in the classroom using regular content materials. Demonstrations should always be followed up with meetings between the demonstrator and the teacher to evaluate the success of the strategy and to discuss

ways the transitions can be made from the demonstration to teacher application.

4. *Observations*. Giving teachers released time to observe in classrooms of other teachers who are applying the techniques successfully can be a very useful way of helping teachers bridge the gap between knowledge and application. Time should be allowed, following the demonstration, for the teachers to discuss methods of successfully applying this strategy in the observing teacher's classroom.

5. *Videotaping*. This can serve as a substitute for both live demonstrations and observations. Videotaping also can provide an opportunity for teachers to review and critique their own use of a strategy and, if desired, discuss the application of the strategy with either a peer or another person providing follow-up assistance.

Making the Transition from Teacher Ability to Established Practice

Inservice sessions often focus their primary effort on objectives related to teacher attitudes and teacher abilities. However, without changes in teacher practices, changes in student behaviors and learnings—the real test of the inservice's value—will never be seen. Therefore, the major goal of follow-up assistance is to insure that objectives in the areas of teacher practices are met so that changes in student behaviors and learnings do actually occur. Without this follow up and the assurance of objectives met in these areas, the inservice sessions may prove to be virtually valueless.

There are a number of ways in which teachers can monitor their own progress in implementing techniques learned in inservice sessions. Stein (1981) provides several excellent suggestions. Fully realizing that teachers find it difficult to "transfer their inservice experiences into the established routines of their classrooms" (p. 524), he suggests use of the "I Will" Planning Chart, which is excerpted from his article and shown here.

The "I Will" chart is designed to be completed by teachers before planning instruction. Used in this manner, the chart serves both to remind teachers of strategies that were presented in the inservice sessions and to encourage them to use those strategies in their lessons. Since each series of inservice sessions will differ based on the needs and interests of participants, the items listed on the "I

Figure 1. The "I Will" planning chart.

Planning for _____ (write name of course)
This week / chapter / unit (circle one) I will work on one skill from each category:

1. Vocabulary	2. Reasoning skills	3. Visual learning	4. Student independent learning
(check one)	(check one)	(check one)	(check one)
Antonyms	Main idea	Photographs	Text reading
Synonyms	Details	Pictures	Vocabulary
Analogies	Conclusion	Graphs	Reasoning from
Words in	Summarization	Maps	reading
context	Author's purpose	Charts	Notetaking
Root words	Cause/effect	Statistics	
Word origins	Fact/opinion	Cartoons	
	Restatement		
	Empathy		

I will use these activities completed during inservice (write in your choices, related to each item checked in the categories above):

Vocabulary	Reasoning skills	Visual learning	Student independent learning
_____	_____	_____	_____
_____	_____	_____	_____
_____	_____	_____	_____
_____	_____	_____	_____

I will use these approaches (check all you will use):
Large group instruction____ Small group work____
Independent study in class____ In-class assignment ____
Homework ____ Testing ____

Will" chart will vary according to the strategies taught in the inservice. The "I Will" chart shown, however, can serve as a model for preparation of a chart which incorporates strategies advocated in the inservice.

Another planning device suggested by Stein is called a "memory window" checklist. This checklist is composed of a series of questions which remind teachers of principles and strategies presented in the workshops that can be applied in their classrooms. Stein's example (1981) of a memory window follows.

Figure 2. "Memory Window" for a reading/viewing/listening lesson.

Before the assignment	Yes	No	Not needed
Will I motivate the students? How?			
Will a purpose for the assignment be established? How?			
Is it necessary to introduce vocabulary? How?			
Shall I link future ideas with previous learning? How?			
During the assignment			
Have I given students a search strategy to use as they encounter information?			
Have I given students a memory strategy?			
After the assignment			
Should I review the vocabulary?			
Shall I seek to develop different levels of understanding, ranging from facts to opinions?			
Is concept integration needed?			
Are there patterns of organization in the information which require a reaction strategy? (cause/effect, conclusions, opinions/facts, author's intentions, comparison/contrast, main idea/detail)			
Do I want students to write about the information they've just acquired?			
In what form? For what audience?			

The "Memory Window" idea should be adapted to reflect the particular inservice topics used; in this way it serves not only as a reminder to implement new strategies, but also as a way to self-monitor their use. Self-monitoring methods, used conscientiously, can increase greatly the use of new strategies, improving the chances that their use will become an established routine.

Coping with Change

Change is difficult. As Vacca and Vacca (1980, p. 28) point out, "the status quo is comfortable; it provides a sense of stability and security." However, inservice education is designed to promote change, to encourage teachers to examine and (possibly) change their beliefs, increase their knowledge, and ultimately modify their practices. Generally, teachers are more willing to change if they are at least somewhat dissatisfied with the status quo. If they perceive that some of their students are having difficulty handling the printed materials used in their content areas and the students' problems result in negative consequences, teachers are more likely to be willing to make changes.

Encouraging teachers to sustain their efforts in making these changes is one of the most difficult tasks of the follow-up person's role. A number of methods may help. First, help teachers set realistic expectations for the changes they are implementing. They should not expect unqualified success with the first attempt. Students do not always adapt well to changes, and fine tuning may be necessary before the new strategies work smoothly and successfully.

Second, be available for problem solving and assistance in modifying plans and activities that are not successful. The follow-up person's support through this difficult time may be crucial in sustaining effort when changes are not initially successful.

Third, make every effort to provide teachers with the types of support listed elsewhere in this chapter. When teachers are attempting changes, factors like peer support, demonstrations, informal meetings, teacher self-monitoring tools, team teaching and shared preparation of activities can all make the process of change easier.

Finally, be sure the follow-up person has and uses the skills and personal characteristics needed for effective follow-up work; these are described in the section that follows.

Interpersonal Skills and Characteristics of Follow-Up Persons

In order to provide successful follow-up assistance, individuals must possess strong interpersonal skills. They must not only have knowledge of the strategies to be applied, but also have experience in successfully applying them. In addition, the person must have the trust and respect of content area teachers. Bean and Wilson (1981) have listed a number of characteristics and skills which reading resource personnel must have if they are to perform their roles effectively. Below are personal characteristics and abilities selected from the Bean and Wilson list which are particularly necessary for a resource person providing follow-up assistance in content area reading.

1. Evidence of both knowledge and skill in using content area reading strategies.

   Content area teachers generally place a high value on experience. They will expect a follow-up person not only to know the reading strategies thoroughly, but also to have had successful experiences applying these strategies in at least one content area, preferably the content area where assistance is being provided. They will expect to be able to draw on these experiences, discussing successes and failures. Samples of study guides, structured overviews, and other materials developed and used with students by the follow-up person, will be extremely useful in helping teachers make the transition from knowledge to established practice. The credibility gained from drawing upon these materials and experiences cannot be underestimated.

2. Ability to communicate effectively with teachers.

   Bean and Wilson (1981) stress the importance of being a good listener with sensitivity to nonverbal as well as verbal communication. In addition, the timing of conversations and choice of locations is an important factor in effective communication. Starting a discussion of how a lesson might be modified while the teacher is monitoring the hall between class periods is obviously poor timing and choice of location. Confidentiality is another factor vitally important to communication. Teachers must feel they can openly discuss not only their successes, but also their failures without hearing about them from others at a later date.

3. Dependability and honesty.

   If assistance is promised, teachers need to know that they can plan on timely, dependable help. Honest, straightforward communication regarding ideas is also important if an open, productive relationship is to exist.

4. Acceptance, genuineness, and sensitivity to the feelings of others.

   Change involves risk taking on the part of teachers; they are unlikely to take these risks if they do not feel they are doing so in a climate of genuine acceptance. The person providing follow-up assistance needs to be aware of: how teachers are reacting to activities, when they are getting discouraged, when they need additional support, and whether communication lines are strong and open.

5. Recognition of the strengths of others and acknowledgement of those strengths.

All people have relative strengths and weaknesses. Recognizing a teacher's relative strengths and guiding the teacher to select strategies which will use these strengths is part of a follow-up person's job. For example, if a teacher has strong conceptual skills and easily sees relationships among ideas, then the use of structured overviews or some other visual representation of the relationship of concepts or ideas would be an excellent choice of strategies. (This assumes, of course, that students need the support of a technique of this sort.)

6. Ability to work effectively with students through demonstrations or team teaching to show how techniques work.

Teachers often need to see a strategy used before they fully understand its use or effectiveness. While follow-up assistance can often be effective without direct contact with students, the ability to demonstrate when needed is quite important. Obviously, prior successful experience using the strategy is imperative; in fact, video tapes of these experiences might serve as a viable substitute for a demonstration if time is limited or direct contact with students is not possible.

Who Provides Follow-Up Assistance?

Follow-up assistance can be provided by various people. The decision of who provides follow up is generally made based on a number of factors including: budgetary considerations, level of administrative commitment, interest of participants in working in peer groups, availability of qualified personnel, and amount and type of follow up needed.

Often the workshop presenter is the best person to provide follow-up assistance. This is especially true if the strategies presented are difficult to apply. The workshop presenter may be the logical choice if there are not others within the school or the district who have successfully used the strategies and can be available for follow-up assistance. However, using the workshop presenter as follow-up person is often not feasible, due either to cost considerations or to scheduling problems. In some situations, using workshop presenters as follow-up people may also not be desirable, especially if the workshop presenter is an outsider and local people are available who can provide the assistance needed. Often a master content area teacher, reading specialist, or district office person may be designated as the inservice coordinator; if so, it may be desirable for this person to provide the follow-up assistance also. The support of the local school principal for use of the strategies often serves as an important incentive to teachers who are considering implementation. Askov and Dupuis (1980) found, one year after a content reading inservice series ended, that the positive effects of the inservice had actually increased at the site where administrative support for content area reading instruction was the strongest. School administrators may provide important encouragement to teachers to implement the strategies recommended at the workshop; however, often they cannot be expected to provide the in-depth follow-up assistance that may be needed.

Peer teachers who have had experience successfully using the techniques make excellent follow-up persons, especially when working with teachers from their own content areas. The opportunity to watch a peer implement a strategy successfully or to hear a peer's enthusiastic support for an idea may make a significant difference in whether area content teachers actually apply strategies presented. The added benefit of having a peer to provide follow-up assistance in implementing a tried and true method may ensure success that otherwise would have been tenuous, at best.

No matter who provides the follow-up assistance it will be necessary to include follow up in the overall inservice plans, either by including funds in the budget to provide for visits from nondistrict personnel or by arranging released time for staff members providing (and those receiving) follow up. If these provisions are not made in advance, follow up is likely to be an afterthought that provides little or no real support to teachers.

References

Askov, E. N., & M. N. Dupuis. "Impact of Content Area Reading Inservice Education on Teachers: A Follow-Up Study Conducted One Year Later," paper presented at the Annual Meeting of the International Reading Association, St. Louis, 1980. (ED 188 140)

Bean, R. M., & R. M. Wilson. *Effecting Change in School Reading Programs: The Resource Role.* Newark, Delaware: International Reading Association, 1981.

Fry, E. B. "Fry's Readability Graph: Clarifications, Validity, and Extension to Level 17," *Journal of Reading*, December 1977, 242-252.

Stein, H. "Building Bridges between Workshops and Content Area Reading Instruction," *Journal of Reading*, March 1981, 523-527.

Vacca, J. L., & R. T. Vacca. "Unfreezing Strategies for Staff Development in Reading," *Reading Teacher*, October 1980, 27-31.

Chapter Eight

Inservice Education for Content Area Teachers: Some Final Thoughts

Mary Dunn Siedow

The challenge of providing inservice education in reading for content area teachers has been the focus of this monograph. As subject specialists, content area teachers have specific needs regarding content area reading which can best be met through inservice education. To meet these special needs of content area teachers, inservice education should be planned with maximum participant involvement and should be organized logically and simply.

As inservice coordinators and committee members use this monograph, they will find that the discussions of each step provide both rationale and resources for content area reading inservice. They will also find themselves using the discussions and the resources as "jumping off" points for ideas from which they can develop successful and effective programs.

The model of inservice education around which this monograph is developed is well suited to content area reading inservice. It is logical and straightforward; it requires the involvement of participants throughout its six steps. It allows for sharing of expertise, for learning by classroom application of strategies demonstrated to be effective. In this final chapter of the monograph the steps of the model will be summarized, some implications for content area reading inservice will be stated, and some hints for implementing the model will be outlined.

The steps of the model are introduced in Chapter 1 and explored in detail in succeeding chapters. The steps are summarized below.

1. *Assessing Needs*

Successful inservice programs begin with needs assessment. A coordinator or committee is named whose job is to determine how and on what topics inservice should be conducted and to oversee the program. Using checklists, surveys, and other means, coordinators or committees can determine participants' needs and can develop inservice programs based on those needs.

2. *Formulating Objectives*

Using needs assessment data and their own good judgment, inservice coordinators or committees formulate program objectives that deserve the best efforts of students and of school personnel and that stand a reasonable chance of being achieved. In each area dealt with in the inservice program, related objectives should be formulated at the levels of teacher beliefs, teacher abilities, teacher practices, student behaviors, and student learnings.

3. *Planning Content*

In planning the actual content to present in initial inservice sessions, coordinators or committees should select instructional strategies that will be 1) viewed as relevant and potentially effective in the classrooms of the teachers being served, 2) easily learned by the teachers, 3) easily blended into regular teaching practices, and 4) likely to show desirable results quickly in classrooms. In planning the content of later inservice sessions, instructional strategies that place more demands on teachers or promise results less quickly can be introduced if those strategies can be clearly seen to capitalize on the strengths of already accepted strategies and to have potential for helping solve pressing problems or for otherwise contributing significantly to student learning.

4. *Selecting Presentation Methods and Staffing*

The methods by which instructional strategies are presented have much to do with insuring that the strategies will be used successfully in classrooms. Demonstrations of strategies followed by opportunities to practice them will 1) help participants see the strategies as relevant and potentially effective and 2) increase participants' confidence and conviction that they can use the strategies effectively. Inservice coordinators or committees may select experienced teachers, consultants, or university personnel as inservice staff, matching individual expertise to the content and strategies to be taught in sessions.

5. *Evaluating Inservice Effectiveness*

Evaluation serves to monitor and document both teachers' and students' growth in knowledge and skills, thus providing important motivation for content inservice participants. Inservice coordinators or committees may also use evaluation to provide ongoing needs assessment, clarifying teachers' and students' needs throughout the inservice process.

6. *Providing Follow-Up Assistance*

Follow-up assistance, a facet often omitted from inservice models, is a critical aspect of this one. Since objectives in the areas of teaching practices and student learnings are very rarely met while workshop series are in progress, inservice coordinators or committees should use follow-up assistance to provide the assurance that these objectives will indeed be met. Long after workshops have ended, follow-up assistance ensures that they have continuing impact.

The implications stated in Chapter 1 should become clear to inservice coordinators and committee members as they read this monograph and begin to develop programs based on the inservice model. The first implication is that like the model, good inservice is interactive; its steps are important in themselves but always must be considered in terms of their interrelationships with each other. Planning and executing successful inservice require that coordinators or committees consider all of the steps in unison even as they work in detail on individual steps. The second implication is that effective inservice must be a long term effort. The design and implementation of a program based on this model is complex and ambitious. To execute a content area reading program based on the model would require commitment over many months. The third implication is that effective inservice in content area reading requires the cooperative involvement of everyone involved—teachers, administrators, supervisors, presenters, coordinators, and committees. Ultimately the most effective inservice situation would be one in which faculty and administrative support is firm, and in which inservice is an ongoing aspect of the total instructional program.

Throughout the pages of this monograph, individual aspects of content area reading inservice have been discussed independently and in relation to one another. Successful inservice programs can be designed based on the ideas in this monograph, and the following hints might facilitate the task of getting started. In addition to using these hints, coordinators and committee members should consult *Guidelines for Successful Reading Staff Development* (Shanker, 1982) for information which complements what has been said here.

1. Remember that although the original impetus for an inservice program might come from teachers, administrators, or supervisors, it is important that someone should take charge of the program. A coordinator or committee should be named early and should take responsibility for overseeing the proceedings. Be sure that these individuals are known to one another and to the teachers who will participate.

2. Obtain the support of administration and the commitment of teachers. Encourage principals and counselors to participate in the inservice program.

3. Move through the steps of the model, developing each section and noting related ideas in other sections. For example, as a needs assessment instrument is developed, think about the kinds of objectives that might be written from its results. As objectives are written, make notes of ways to evaluate them. As content for sessions is identified, consider what kinds of methods and staff will present it most effectively.

5. Have a preliminary plan for the total program before beginning. Be flexible in using this plan. Adapt and modify the plan or parts of it as needed.

6. As the inservice program progresses, keep up the cooperative enthusiasm of participants. Continue the use of motivational strategies well into the follow-up phase of the program.

This monograph ends as it began—with a statement that content area teachers are special people who have needs and desires to learn about content area reading; needs and desires which can be met effectively through inservice education. This monograph has been written to provide those in charge of content area reading inservice with resources they can use in developing successful programs.

Reference

Shanker, James L. *Guidelines for Successful Reading Staff Development*. Newark, Delaware: International Reading Association, 1982.